D1509765

The Law School Admission Council (LSAC) is a nonprofit corporation that provides unique, state-of-the-art admission products and services to ease the admission process for law schools and their applicants worldwide. Currently, 220 law schools in the United States, Canada, and Australia are members of the Council and benefit from LSAC's services.

LSAC fees, policies, and procedures relating to, but not limited to, test registration, test administration, test score reporting, misconduct and irregularities, Credential Assembly Service (CAS), and other matters may change without notice at any time. Up-to-date LSAC policies and procedures are available at LSAC.org.

ISBN-13: 978-0-9860455-3-0

Print number
10 9 8 7 6 5 4 3 2 1

TABLE OF CONTENTS

INTRODUCTION TO THE LSAT

The Law School Admission Test is a half-day standardized test required for admission to all ABA-approved law schools, most Canadian law schools, and many other law schools. It consists of five 35-minute sections of multiple-choice questions. Four of the five sections contribute to the test taker's score. These sections include one Reading Comprehension section, one Analytical Reasoning section, and two Logical Reasoning sections. The unscored section, commonly referred to as the variable section, typically is used to pretest new test questions or to preequate new test forms. The placement of this section in the LSAT will vary. A 35-minute writing sample is administered at the end of the test. The writing sample is not scored by LSAC, but copies are sent to all law schools to which you apply. The score scale for the LSAT is 120 to 180.

The LSAT is designed to measure skills considered essential for success in law school: the reading and comprehension of complex texts with accuracy and insight; the organization and management of information and the ability to draw reasonable inferences from it; the ability to think critically; and the analysis and evaluation of the reasoning and arguments of others.

The LSAT provides a standard measure of acquired reading and verbal reasoning skills that law schools can use as one of several factors in assessing applicants.

For up-to-date information about LSAC's services, go to our website, LSAC.org.

SCORING

Your LSAT score is based on the number of questions you answer correctly (the raw score). There is no deduction for incorrect answers, and all questions count equally. In other words, there is no penalty for guessing.

Test Score Accuracy—Reliability and Standard Error of Measurement

Candidates perform at different levels on different occasions for reasons quite unrelated to the characteristics of a test itself. The accuracy of test scores is best described by the use of two related statistical terms: reliability and standard error of measurement.

Reliability is a measure of how consistently a test measures the skills being assessed. The higher the reliability coefficient for a test, the more certain we can be that test takers would get very similar scores if they took the test again.

LSAC reports an internal consistency measure of reliability for every test form. Reliability can vary from 0.00 to 1.00, and a test with no measurement error would have a reliability coefficient of 1.00 (never attained in practice). Reliability coefficients for past LSAT forms have ranged from .90 to .95, indicating a high degree of consistency for these tests. LSAC expects the reliability of the LSAT to continue to fall within the same range.

LSAC also reports the amount of measurement error associated with each test form, a concept known as the standard error of measurement (SEM). The SEM, which is usually about 2.6 points, indicates how close a test taker's observed score is likely to be to his or her true score. True scores are theoretical scores that would be obtained from perfectly reliable tests with no measurement error—scores never known in practice.

Score bands, or ranges of scores that contain a test taker's true score a certain percentage of the time, can be derived using the SEM. LSAT score bands are constructed by adding and subtracting the (rounded) SEM to and from an actual LSAT score (e.g., the LSAT score, plus or minus 3 points). Scores near 120 or 180 have asymmetrical bands. Score bands constructed in this manner will contain an individual's true score approximately 68 percent of the time.

Measurement error also must be taken into account when comparing LSAT scores of two test takers. It is likely that small differences in scores are due to measurement error rather than to meaningful differences in ability. The standard error of score differences provides some guidance as to the importance of differences between two scores. The standard error of score differences is approximately 1.4 times larger than the standard error of measurement for the individual scores.

Thus, a test score should be regarded as a useful but approximate measure of a test taker's abilities as measured by the test, not as an exact determination of his or her abilities. LSAC encourages law schools to examine the range of scores within the interval that probably contains the test taker's true score (e.g., the test taker's score band) rather than solely interpret the reported score alone.

Adjustments for Variation in Test Difficulty

All test forms of the LSAT reported on the same score scale are designed to measure the same abilities, but one test form may be slightly easier or more difficult than another. The scores from different test forms are made comparable through a statistical procedure known as equating. As a result of equating, a given scaled score earned on different test forms reflects the same level of ability.

Research on the LSAT

Summaries of LSAT validity studies and other LSAT research can be found in member law school libraries and at LSAC.org.

To Inquire About Test Questions

If you find what you believe to be an error or ambiguity in a test question that affects your response to the question, contact LSAC by e-mail: LSATTS@LSAC.org, or write to Law School Admission Council, Test Development Group, PO Box 40, Newtown, PA 18940-0040.

HOW THIS PREPTEST DIFFERS FROM AN ACTUAL LSAT

This PrepTest is made up of the scored sections and writing sample from the actual disclosed LSAT administered in September 2014. However, it does not contain the extra, variable section that is used to pretest new test items of one of the three multiple-choice question types. The three multiple-choice question types may be in a different order in an actual LSAT than in this PrepTest. This is because the order of these question types is intentionally varied for each administration of the test.

THE THREE LSAT MULTIPLE-CHOICE QUESTION TYPES

The multiple-choice questions that make up most of the LSAT reflect a broad range of academic disciplines and are intended to give no advantage to candidates from a particular academic background.

The five sections of the test contain three different question types. The following material presents a general discussion of the nature of each question type and some strategies that can be used in answering them.

Analytical Reasoning Questions

Analytical Reasoning questions are designed to assess the ability to consider a group of facts and rules, and, given those facts and rules, determine what could or must be true. The specific scenarios associated with these questions are usually unrelated to law, since they are intended to be accessible to a wide range of test takers. However, the skills tested parallel those involved in determining what could or must be the case given a set of regulations, the terms of a contract, or the facts of a legal case in relation to the law. In Analytical Reasoning questions, you are asked to reason deductively from a set of statements and rules or principles that describe relationships among persons, things, or events.

Analytical Reasoning questions appear in sets, with each set based on a single passage. The passage used for each set of questions describes common ordering relationships or grouping relationships, or a combination of both types of relationships. Examples include scheduling employees for work shifts, assigning instructors to class sections, ordering tasks according to priority, and distributing grants for projects.

Analytical Reasoning questions test a range of deductive reasoning skills. These include:

- Comprehending the basic structure of a set of relationships by determining a complete solution to the problem posed (for example, an acceptable seating arrangement of all six diplomats around a table)

- Reasoning with conditional ("if-then") statements and recognizing logically equivalent formulations of such statements

- Inferring what could be true or must be true from given facts and rules

- Inferring what could be true or must be true from given facts and rules together with new information in the form of an additional or substitute fact or rule

- Recognizing when two statements are logically equivalent in context by identifying a condition or rule that could replace one of the original conditions while still resulting in the same possible outcomes

Analytical Reasoning questions reflect the kinds of detailed analyses of relationships and sets of constraints that a law student must perform in legal problem solving. For example, an Analytical Reasoning passage might describe six diplomats being seated around a table, following certain rules of protocol as to who can sit where. You, the test taker, must answer questions about the logical implications of given and new information. For example, you may be asked who can sit between diplomats X and Y, or who cannot sit next to X if W sits next to Y. Similarly, if you were a student in law school, you might be asked to analyze a scenario involving a set of particular circumstances and a set of governing rules in the form of constitutional provisions, statutes, administrative codes, or prior rulings that have been upheld. You might then be asked to determine the legal options in the scenario: what is required given the scenario, what is permissible given the scenario, and what is prohibited given the scenario. Or you might be asked to develop a "theory" for the case: when faced with an incomplete set of facts about the case, you must fill in the picture based on what is implied by the facts that are known. The problem could be elaborated by the addition of new information or hypotheticals.

No formal training in logic is required to answer these questions correctly. Analytical Reasoning questions are intended to be answered using knowledge, skills, and reasoning ability generally expected of college students and graduates.

Suggested Approach

Some people may prefer to answer first those questions about a passage that seem less difficult and then those that seem more difficult. In general, it is best to finish one passage before starting on another, because much time can be lost in returning to a passage and reestablishing familiarity with its relationships. However, if you are having great difficulty on one particular set of questions and are spending too much time on them, it may be to your advantage to skip that set of questions and go on to the next passage, returning to the problematic set of questions after you have finished the other questions in the section.

Do not assume that because the conditions for a set of questions look long or complicated, the questions based on those conditions will be especially difficult.

Read the passage carefully. Careful reading and analysis are necessary to determine the exact nature of the relationships involved in an Analytical Reasoning passage. Some relationships are fixed (for example, P and R must always work on the same project). Other relationships are variable (for example, Q must be assigned to either team 1 or team 3). Some relationships that are not stated explicitly in the conditions are implied by and can be deduced from those that are stated (for example, if one condition about paintings in a display specifies that Painting K must be to the left of Painting Y, and another specifies that Painting W must be to the left of Painting K, then it can be deduced that Painting W must be to the left of Painting Y).

In reading the conditions, do not introduce unwarranted assumptions. For instance, in a set of questions establishing relationships of height and weight among the members of a team, do not assume that a person who is taller than another person must weigh more than that person. As another example, suppose a set involves ordering and a question in the set asks what must be true if both X and Y must be earlier than Z; in this case, do not assume that X must be earlier than Y merely because X is mentioned before Y. All the information needed to answer each question is provided in the passage and the question itself.

The conditions are designed to be as clear as possible. Do not interpret the conditions as if they were intended to trick you. For example, if a question asks how many people could be eligible to serve on a committee, consider only those people named in the passage unless directed otherwise. When in doubt, read the conditions in their most obvious sense. Remember, however, that the language in the conditions is intended to be read for precise meaning. It is essential to pay particular attention to words that describe or limit relationships, such as "only," "exactly," "never," "always," "must be," "cannot be," and the like.

The result of this careful reading will be a clear picture of the structure of the relationships involved, including the kinds of relationships permitted, the participants in the relationships, and the range of possible actions or attributes for these participants.

Keep in mind question independence. Each question should be considered separately from the other questions in its set. No information, except what is given in the original conditions, should be carried over from one question to another.

In some cases a question will simply ask for conclusions to be drawn from the conditions as originally given. Some questions may, however, add information to the original conditions or temporarily suspend or replace one of the original conditions for the purpose of that question only. For example, if Question 1 adds the supposition "if P is sitting at table 2 ...," this supposition should NOT be carried over to any other question in the set.

Consider highlighting text and using diagrams. Many people find it useful to underline key points in the passage and in each question. In addition, it may prove very helpful to draw a diagram to assist you in finding the solution to the problem.

In preparing for the test, you may wish to experiment with different types of diagrams. For a scheduling problem, a simple calendar-like diagram may be helpful. For a grouping problem, an array of labeled columns or rows may be useful.

Even though most people find diagrams to be very helpful, some people seldom use them, and for some individual questions no one will need a diagram. There is by no means universal agreement on which kind of diagram is best for which problem or in which cases a diagram is most useful. Do not be concerned if a particular problem in the test seems to be best approached without the use of a diagram.

Logical Reasoning Questions

Arguments are a fundamental part of the law, and analyzing arguments is a key element of legal analysis. Training in the law builds on a foundation of basic reasoning skills. Law students must draw on the skills of analyzing, evaluating, constructing, and refuting arguments. They need to be able to identify what information is relevant to an issue or argument and what impact further evidence might have. They need to be able to reconcile opposing positions and use arguments to persuade others.

Logical Reasoning questions evaluate the ability to analyze, critically evaluate, and complete arguments as they occur in ordinary language. The questions are based on short arguments drawn from a wide variety of sources, including newspapers, general interest magazines, scholarly publications, advertisements, and informal discourse. These arguments mirror legal reasoning in the types of arguments presented and in their complexity, though few of the arguments actually have law as a subject matter.

Each Logical Reasoning question requires you to read and comprehend a short passage, then answer one question (or, rarely, two questions) about it. The questions are designed to assess a wide range of skills involved in thinking critically, with an emphasis on skills that are central to legal reasoning.

These skills include:

- Recognizing the parts of an argument and their relationships

- Recognizing similarities and differences between patterns of reasoning

- Drawing well-supported conclusions

- Reasoning by analogy

- Recognizing misunderstandings or points of disagreement

- Determining how additional evidence affects an argument

- Detecting assumptions made by particular arguments

- Identifying and applying principles or rules

- Identifying flaws in arguments

- Identifying explanations

The questions do not presuppose specialized knowledge of logical terminology. For example, you will not be expected to know the meaning of specialized terms such as "ad hominem" or "syllogism." On the other hand, you will be expected to understand and critique the reasoning contained in arguments. This requires that you possess a university-level understanding of widely used concepts such as argument, premise, assumption, and conclusion.

Suggested Approach

Read each question carefully. Make sure that you understand the meaning of each part of the question. Make sure that you understand the meaning of each answer choice and the ways in which it may or may not relate to the question posed.

Do not pick a response simply because it is a true statement. Although true, it may not answer the question posed.

Answer each question on the basis of the information that is given, even if you do not agree with it. Work within the context provided by the passage. LSAT questions do not involve any tricks or hidden meanings.

Reading Comprehension Questions

Both law school and the practice of law revolve around extensive reading of highly varied, dense, argumentative, and expository texts (for example, cases, codes, contracts, briefs, decisions, evidence). This reading must be exacting, distinguishing precisely what is said from what is not said. It involves comparison, analysis, synthesis, and application (for example, of principles and rules). It involves drawing appropriate inferences and applying ideas and arguments to new contexts. Law school reading also requires the ability to grasp unfamiliar subject matter and the ability to penetrate difficult and challenging material.

The purpose of LSAT Reading Comprehension questions is to measure the ability to read, with understanding and insight, examples of lengthy and complex materials similar to those commonly encountered in law school. The Reading Comprehension section of the LSAT contains four sets of reading questions, each set consisting of a selection of reading material followed by five to eight questions. The reading selection in three of the four sets consists of a single reading passage; the other set contains two related shorter passages. Sets with two passages are a variant of Reading Comprehension called Comparative Reading, which was introduced in June 2007.

Comparative Reading questions concern the relationships between the two passages, such as those of generalization/instance, principle/application, or point/counterpoint. Law school work often requires reading two or more texts in conjunction with each other and understanding their relationships. For example, a law student may read a trial court decision together with an appellate court decision that overturns it, or identify the fact pattern from a hypothetical suit together with the potentially controlling case law.

Reading selections for LSAT Reading Comprehension questions are drawn from a wide range of subjects in the humanities, the social sciences, the biological and physical sciences, and areas related to the law. Generally, the selections are densely written, use high-level vocabulary, and contain sophisticated argument or complex rhetorical structure (for example, multiple points of view). Reading Comprehension questions require you to read carefully and accurately, to determine the relationships among the various parts of the reading selection, and to draw reasonable inferences from the material in the selection. The questions may ask about the following characteristics of a passage or pair of passages:

- The main idea or primary purpose

- Information that is explicitly stated

- Information or ideas that can be inferred

- The meaning or purpose of words or phrases as used in context

- The organization or structure

- The application of information in the selection to a new context

- Principles that function in the selection

- Analogies to claims or arguments in the selection

- An author's attitude as revealed in the tone of a passage or the language used

- The impact of new information on claims or arguments in the selection

Suggested Approach

Since reading selections are drawn from many different disciplines and sources, you should not be discouraged if you encounter material with which you are not familiar. It is important to remember that questions are to be answered exclusively on the basis of the information provided in the selection. There is no particular knowledge that you are expected to bring to the test, and you should not make inferences based on any prior knowledge of a subject that you may have. You may, however, wish to defer working on a set of questions that seems particularly difficult or unfamiliar until after you have dealt with sets you find easier.

Strategies. One question that often arises in connection with Reading Comprehension has to do with the most effective and efficient order in which to read the selections and questions. Possible approaches include:

- reading the selection very closely and then answering the questions;

- reading the questions first, reading the selection closely, and then returning to the questions; or

- skimming the selection and questions very quickly, then rereading the selection closely and answering the questions.

Test takers are different, and the best strategy for one might not be the best strategy for another. In preparing for the test, therefore, you might want to experiment with the different strategies and decide what works most effectively for you.

Remember that your strategy must be effective under timed conditions. For this reason, the first strategy— reading the selection very closely and then answering the questions—may be the most effective for you. Nonetheless, if you believe that one of the other strategies

might be more effective for you, you should try it out and assess your performance using it.

Reading the selection. Whatever strategy you choose, you should give the passage or pair of passages at least one careful reading before answering the questions. Try to distinguish main ideas from supporting ideas, and opinions or attitudes from factual, objective information. Note transitions from one idea to the next and identify the relationships among the different ideas or parts of a passage, or between the two passages in Comparative Reading sets. Consider how and why an author makes points and draws conclusions. Be sensitive to implications of what the passages say.

You may find it helpful to mark key parts of passages. For example, you might underline main ideas or important arguments, and you might circle transitional words— "although," "nevertheless," "correspondingly," and the like—that will help you map the structure of a passage. Also, you might note descriptive words that will help you identify an author's attitude toward a particular idea or person.

Answering the Questions

- Always read all the answer choices before selecting the best answer. The best answer choice is the one that most accurately and completely answers the question being posed.

- Respond to the specific question being asked. Do not pick an answer choice simply because it is a true statement. For example, picking a true statement might yield an incorrect answer to a question in which you are asked to identify an author's position on an issue, since you are not being asked to evaluate the truth of the author's position but only to correctly identify what that position is.

- Answer the questions only on the basis of the information provided in the selection. Your own views, interpretations, or opinions, and those you have heard from others, may sometimes conflict with those expressed in a reading selection; however, you are expected to work within the context provided by the reading selection. You should not expect to agree with everything you encounter in Reading Comprehension passages.

THE WRITING SAMPLE

On the day of the test, you will be asked to write one sample essay. LSAC does not score the writing sample, but copies are sent to all law schools to which you apply. According to a 2006 LSAC survey of 157 United States and Canadian law schools, almost all use the writing sample in evaluating at least some applications for admission. Failure to respond to writing sample prompts and frivolous responses have been used by law schools as grounds for rejection of applications for admission.

In developing and implementing the writing sample portion of the LSAT, LSAC has operated on the following premises: First, law schools and the legal profession value highly the ability to communicate effectively in writing. Second, it is important to encourage potential law students to develop effective writing skills. Third, a sample of an applicant's writing, produced under controlled conditions, is a potentially useful indication of that person's writing ability. Fourth, the writing sample can serve as an independent check on other writing submitted by applicants as part of the admission process. Finally, writing samples may be useful for diagnostic purposes related to improving a candidate's writing.

The writing prompt presents a decision problem. You are asked to make a choice between two positions or courses of action. Both of the choices are defensible, and you are given criteria and facts on which to base your decision. There is no "right" or "wrong" position to take on the topic, so the quality of each test taker's response is a function not of which choice is made, but of how well or poorly the choice is supported and how well or poorly the other choice is criticized.

The LSAT writing prompt was designed and validated by legal education professionals. Since it involves writing based on fact sets and criteria, the writing sample gives applicants the opportunity to demonstrate the type of argumentative writing that is required in law school, although the topics are usually nonlegal.

You will have 35 minutes in which to plan and write an essay on the topic you receive. Read the topic and the accompanying directions carefully. You will probably find it best to spend a few minutes considering the topic and organizing your thoughts before you begin writing. In your essay, be sure to develop your ideas fully, leaving time, if possible, to review what you have written. Do not write on a topic other than the one specified. Writing on a topic of your own choice is not acceptable.

No special knowledge is required or expected for this writing exercise. Law schools are interested in the reasoning, clarity, organization, language usage, and writing mechanics displayed in your essay. How well you write is more important than how much you write. Confine your essay to the blocked, lined area on the front and back of the separate Writing Sample Response Sheet. Only that area will be reproduced for law schools. Be sure that your writing is legible.

TAKING THE PREPTEST UNDER SIMULATED LSAT CONDITIONS

One important way to prepare for the LSAT is to simulate the day of the test by taking a practice test under actual time constraints. Taking a practice test under timed conditions helps you to estimate the amount of time you can afford to spend on each question in a section and to determine the question types on which you may need additional practice.

Since the LSAT is a timed test, it is important to use your allotted time wisely. During the test, you may work only on the section designated by the test supervisor. You cannot devote extra time to a difficult section and make up that time on a section you find easier. In pacing yourself, and checking your answers, you should think of each section of the test as a separate minitest.

Be sure that you answer every question on the test. When you do not know the correct answer to a question, first eliminate the responses that you know are incorrect, then make your best guess among the remaining choices. Do not be afraid to guess as there is no penalty for incorrect answers.

When you take a practice test, abide by all the requirements specified in the directions and keep strictly within the specified time limits. Work without a rest period. When you take an actual test, you will have only a short break—usually 10–15 minutes—after SECTION III.

When taken under conditions as much like actual testing conditions as possible, a practice test provides very useful preparation for taking the LSAT.

Official directions for the four multiple-choice sections and the writing sample are included in this PrepTest so that you can approximate actual testing conditions as you practice.

To take the test:

- Set a timer for 35 minutes. Answer all the questions in SECTION I of this PrepTest. Stop working on that section when the 35 minutes have elapsed.

- Repeat, allowing yourself 35 minutes each for sections II, III, and IV.

- Set the timer again for 35 minutes, then prepare your response to the writing sample topic at the end of this PrepTest.

- Refer to "Computing Your Score" for the PrepTest for instruction on evaluating your performance. An answer key is provided for that purpose.

The practice test that follows consists of four sections corresponding to the four scored sections of the September 2014 LSAT. Also reprinted is the September 2014 unscored writing sample topic.

General Directions for the LSAT Answer Sheet

The actual testing time for this portion of the test will be 2 hours 55 minutes. There are five sections, each with a time limit of 35 minutes. The supervisor will tell you when to begin and end each section. If you finish a section before time is called, you may check your work on that section **only;** do not turn to any other section of the test book and do not work on any other section either in the test book or on the answer sheet.

There are several different types of questions on the test, and each question type has its own directions. **Be sure you understand the directions for each question type before attempting to answer any questions in that section.**

Not everyone will finish all the questions in the time allowed. Do not hurry, but work steadily and as quickly as you can without sacrificing accuracy. You are advised to use your time effectively. If a question seems too difficult, go on to the next one and return to the difficult question after completing the section. **MARK THE BEST ANSWER YOU CAN FOR EVERY QUESTION. NO DEDUCTIONS WILL BE MADE FOR WRONG ANSWERS. YOUR SCORE WILL BE BASED ONLY ON THE NUMBER OF QUESTIONS YOU ANSWER CORRECTLY.**

ALL YOUR ANSWERS MUST BE MARKED ON THE ANSWER SHEET. Answer spaces for each question are lettered to correspond with the letters of the potential answers to each question in the test book. After you have decided which of the answers is correct, blacken the corresponding space on the answer sheet. **BE SURE THAT EACH MARK IS BLACK AND COMPLETELY FILLS THE ANSWER SPACE.** Give only one answer to each question. If you change an answer, be sure that all previous marks are **erased completely.** Since the answer sheet is machine scored, incomplete erasures may be interpreted as intended answers. **ANSWERS RECORDED IN THE TEST BOOK WILL NOT BE SCORED.**

There may be more question numbers on this answer sheet than there are questions in a section. Do not be concerned, but be certain that the section and number of the question you are answering matches the answer sheet section and question number. Additional answer spaces in any answer sheet section should be left blank. Begin your next section in the number one answer space for that section.

LSAC takes various steps to ensure that answer sheets are returned from test centers in a timely manner for processing. In the unlikely event that an answer sheet is not received, LSAC will permit the examinee either to retest at no additional fee or to receive a refund of his or her LSAT fee. **THESE REMEDIES ARE THE ONLY REMEDIES AVAILABLE IN THE UNLIKELY EVENT THAT AN ANSWER SHEET IS NOT RECEIVED BY LSAC.**

Score Cancellation

Complete this section only if you are absolutely certain you want to cancel your score. **A CANCELLATION REQUEST CANNOT BE RESCINDED. IF YOU ARE AT ALL UNCERTAIN, YOU SHOULD NOT COMPLETE THIS SECTION.**

To cancel your score from this administration, you **must:**

A. fill in both ovals here ...... ○ ○
          AND
B. read the following statement. Then sign your name and enter the date.
YOUR SIGNATURE ALONE IS NOT SUFFICIENT FOR SCORE CANCELLATION. BOTH OVALS ABOVE MUST BE FILLED IN FOR SCANNING EQUIPMENT TO RECOGNIZE YOUR REQUEST FOR SCORE CANCELLATION.

I certify that I wish to cancel my test score from this administration. I understand that my request is irreversible and that my score will not be sent to me or to the law schools to which I apply.

Sign your name in full
_____

Date
_____

HOW DID YOU PREPARE FOR THE LSAT?
(Select all that apply.)

Responses to this item are voluntary and will be used for statistical research purposes only.

- ○ By studying the free sample questions available on LSAC's website.
- ○ By taking the free sample LSAT available on LSAC's website.
- ○ By working through official LSAT *PrepTests*, *ItemWise*, and/or other LSAC test prep products.
- ○ By using LSAT prep books or software **not** published by LSAC.
- ○ By attending a commercial test preparation or coaching course.
- ○ By attending a test preparation or coaching course offered through an undergraduate institution.
- ○ Self study.
- ○ Other preparation.
- ○ No preparation.

CERTIFYING STATEMENT

Please write the following statement. Sign and date.

I certify that I am the examinee whose name appears on this answer sheet and that I am here to take the LSAT for the sole purpose of being considered for admission to law school. I further certify that I will neither assist nor receive assistance from any other candidate, and I agree not to copy, retain, or transmit examination questions in any form or discuss them with any other person.

_____
_____
_____
_____
_____
_____
_____
_____

SIGNATURE: _____   TODAY'S DATE: ___/___/___
                                                            MONTH DAY YEAR

INSTRUCTIONS FOR COMPLETING THE BIOGRAPHICAL AREA ARE ON THE BACK COVER OF YOUR TEST BOOKLET.
USE ONLY A NO. 2 OR HB PENCIL TO COMPLETE THIS ANSWER SHEET. DO NOT USE INK.

1 LAST NAME · FIRST NAME · MI

2 LAST 4 DIGITS OF SOCIAL SECURITY/ SOCIAL INSURANCE NO.

3 LSAC ACCOUNT NUMBER

4 CENTER NUMBER

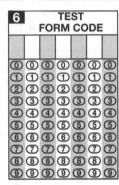

5 DATE OF BIRTH

MONTH	DAY	YEAR
○ Jan		
○ Feb		
○ Mar		
○ Apr		
○ May		
○ June		
○ July		
○ Aug		
○ Sept		
○ Oct		
○ Nov		
○ Dec		

6 TEST FORM CODE

7 RACIAL/ETHNIC DESCRIPTION
Mark one or more
- ○ 1 Amer. Indian/Alaska Native
- ○ 2 Asian
- ○ 3 Black/African American
- ○ 4 Canadian Aboriginal
- ○ 5 Caucasian/White
- ○ 6 Hispanic/Latino
- ○ 7 Native Hawaiian/ Other Pacific Islander
- ○ 8 Puerto Rican
- ○ 9 TSI/Aboriginal Australia

8 GENDER
- ○ Male
- ○ Female

9 DOMINANT LANGUAGE
- ○ English
- ○ Other

10 ENGLISH FLUENCY
- ○ Yes
- ○ No

11 TEST DATE
____ / ____ / ____
MONTH   DAY   YEAR

12 TEST FORM

Law School Admission Test

Mark one and only one answer to each question. Be sure to fill in completely the space for your intended answer choice. If you erase, do so completely. Make no stray marks.

13 TEST BOOK SERIAL NO.

SECTION 1 · **SECTION 2** · **SECTION 3** · **SECTION 4** · **SECTION 5**

Each section: questions 1–30, answer choices A B C D E

14 PLEASE PRINT INFORMATION

LAST NAME

FIRST NAME

DATE OF BIRTH

A

THE PREPTEST

SECTION I

Time—35 minutes

27 Questions

<u>Directions:</u> Each set of questions in this section is based on a single passage or a pair of passages. The questions are to be answered on the basis of what is <u>stated</u> or <u>implied</u> in the passage or pair of passages. For some of the questions, more than one of the choices could conceivably answer the question. However, you are to choose the <u>best</u> answer; that is, the response that most accurately and completely answers the question, and blacken the corresponding space on your answer sheet.

Charles Darwin objected to all attempts to reduce his theory of evolution to its doctrine of natural selection. "Natural selection has been the main but not the exclusive means of modification," he declared.
(5) Nonetheless, a group of self-proclaimed strict constructionist Darwinians has recently risen to prominence by reducing Darwin's theory in just this way. These theorists use the mechanism of natural selection to explain all biological phenomena; they
(10) assert that natural selection is responsible for every aspect of every species' form and behavior, and for the success or failure of species in general.

Natural selection is generally held to result in adaptation, the shaping of an organism's form and
(15) behavior in response to environmental conditions to achieve enhanced reproductive success. If the strict constructionists are right, the persistence of every attribute and the survival of every species are due to such adaptation. But in fact, nature provides numerous
(20) examples of attributes that are not adaptations for reproductive success and of species whose success or failure had little to do with their adaptations.

For example, while it is true that some random mutations of genetic material produce attributes that
(25) enhance reproductive success and are thus favored by natural selection, and others produce harmful attributes that are weeded out, we now know from population genetics that most mutations fall into neither category. Research has revealed that neutral, nonadaptive
(30) changes account to a large extent for the evolution of DNA. Most substitutions of one unit of DNA for another within a population have no effect on reproductive success. These alterations often change the attributes of species, but their persistence from
(35) one generation to the next is not explainable by natural selection.

Additionally, the study of mass extinctions in paleontology has undermined the strict constructionist claim that natural selection can account for every
(40) species' success or failure. The extinction of the dinosaurs some 65 million years ago was probably caused by the impact of an extraterrestrial body. Smaller animal species are generally better able to survive the catastrophic changes in climate that we
(45) would expect to follow from such an impact, and mammals in the Cretaceous period were quite small because they could not compete on the large scale of the dominant dinosaurs. But while this scenario explains why dinosaurs died off and mammals fared
(50) relatively well, it does not conform to the strict constructionist view of the adaptive reasons for the success of species. For that view assumes that adaptations are a response to conditions that are already in place at the time the adaptations occur,
(55) and mammals could not have adapted in advance to conditions caused by the impact. In a sense, their success was the result of dumb luck.

1. Which one of the following most accurately expresses the main point of the passage?

(A) Evidence from two areas of science undermines the strict constructionist claim that natural selection is the only driving force behind evolution.

(B) According to strict constructionist Darwinians, new evidence suggests that natural selection is responsible for the failure of most extinct species.

(C) New evidence demonstrates that natural selection can produce nonadaptive as well as adaptive changes.

(D) Strict constructionist followers of Darwin maintain that natural selection is responsible for all evolutionary change.

(E) Evidence from the study of population genetics helps to disprove the claim that natural selection results in the survival of the fittest species.

2. According to the author, mammals were able to survive catastrophic environmental changes that occurred roughly 65 million years ago because they

(A) had adapted previously to similar changes
(B) were relatively small
(C) were highly intelligent
(D) lived in a wide range of environments
(E) were able to reproduce quickly

GO ON TO THE NEXT PAGE.

3. The author asserts which one of the following regarding mutations of genetic material?

   (A) The majority of such mutations are not passed on to subsequent generations.
   (B) The majority of such mutations occur during periods when mass extinctions take place.
   (C) The majority of such mutations change species' behavior rather than their appearance.
   (D) The majority of such mutations have no effect on reproductive success.
   (E) The majority of such mutations occur in larger rather than smaller species.

4. The author would be most likely to agree with which one of the following statements?

   (A) Natural selection is responsible for almost none of the characteristics of existing species.
   (B) The fact that a species flourishes in a certain environment is not proof of its adaptation to that environment.
   (C) Only evolutionary changes that provide some advantage to a species are transmitted to subsequent generations.
   (D) Large animal species are generally unable to survive in harsh environmental conditions.
   (E) Natural selection is useful for explaining the form but not the behavior of most species.

5. The author's stance toward the arguments of the strict constructionist Darwinians can most accurately be described as one of

   (A) emphatic disagreement
   (B) mild disapproval
   (C) open-minded neutrality
   (D) conditional agreement
   (E) unreserved endorsement

6. Which one of the following most accurately and completely describes the function of the second paragraph of the passage?

   (A) It outlines the objections to traditional evolutionary theory raised by the strict constructionists mentioned in the first paragraph.
   (B) It lists recent evidence suggesting that the strict constructionist claims described in the first paragraph are incorrect.
   (C) It describes the strict constructionists' view of evolutionary theory in order to explain why the evidence described in subsequent paragraphs has recently gotten so much attention.
   (D) It enumerates the arguments for the strict constructionist position that are rebutted in the paragraphs that follow.
   (E) It explains the ramifications of the strict constructionists' claims and helps clarify the relevance of evidence offered in subsequent paragraphs.

7. The primary purpose of the passage is to

   (A) argue in favor of a recently proposed hypothesis
   (B) summarize a contemporary debate
   (C) demonstrate that a particular view is incorrect
   (D) criticize the proponents of a traditional theory
   (E) explain why a particular theory is gaining popularity

GO ON TO THE NEXT PAGE.

From a critical discussion of the work of Victorian photographer Julia Margaret Cameron.

What Cameron called her "fancy-subject" pictures—photographs in which two or more costumed sitters enacted, under Cameron's direction, scenes from the Bible, mythology, Shakespeare, or Tennyson—
(5) bear unmistakable traces of the often comical conditions under which they were taken. In many respects they have more connection to the family album pictures of recalcitrant relatives who have been herded together for the obligatory group picture than they do to the
(10) masterpieces of Western painting. In Raphael and Giotto there are no infant Christs whose faces are blurred because they moved, or who are looking at the viewer with frank hatred. These traces, of course, are what give the photographs their life and charm. If
(15) Cameron had succeeded in her project of making seamless works of illustrative art, her work would be among the curiosities of Victorian photography—like Oscar Gustave Rejlander's extravagantly awful *The Two Ways of Life*—rather than among its most
(20) vital images.

It is precisely the camera's realism—its stubborn obsession with the surface of things—that has given Cameron's theatricality and artificiality its atmosphere of truth. It is the truth of the sitting, rather than the
(25) fiction which all the dressing up was in aid of, that wafts out of these wonderful and strange, not-quite-in-focus photographs. They are what they are: pictures of housemaids and nieces and husbands and village children who are dressed up as Mary Madonnas and
(30) infant Jesuses and John the Baptists and Lancelots and Guineveres and trying desperately hard to sit still. The way each sitter endures his or her ordeal is the collective action of the photograph, its "plot" so to speak. When we look at a narrative painting we can
(35) suspend our disbelief; when we look at a narrative photograph we cannot. We are always aware of the photograph's doubleness—of each figure's imaginary and real personas. Theater can transcend its doubleness, can make us believe (for at least some of the time) that
(40) we are seeing only Lear or Medea. Still photographs of theatrical scenes can never escape being pictures of actors.

What gives Cameron's pictures of actors their special quality—their status as treasures of photography of an unfathomably peculiar sort—is their singular
(45) combination of amateurism and artistry. In *The Passing of Arthur*, for example, the mast and oar of the makeshift boat representing a royal barge are obviously broomsticks and the water is white muslin
(50) drapery. But these details are insignificant. For once, the homely truth of the sitting gives right of place to the romantic fantasy of its director. The picture, a night scene, is magical and mysterious. While Cameron's fancy-subject pictures have been compared
(55) to poor amateur theatricals, *The Passing of Arthur* puts one in mind of good amateur theatricals one has seen, and recalls with shameless delight.

8. Which one of the following most accurately expresses the main point of the passage?

(A) The circumstances under which Cameron's fancy-subject pictures were taken render them unintentionally comical.

(B) The peculiar charm of Cameron's fancy-subject pictures derives from the viewer's simultaneous awareness of the fictional scene portrayed and the circumstances of its portrayal.

(C) The implicit claim of Cameron's fancy-subject pictures to comparison with the masterpieces of Western painting is undermined by the obtrusiveness of the sitters.

(D) The most successful of Cameron's fancy-subject pictures from an aesthetic point of view are those in which the viewer is completely unaware that the sitters are engaged in role playing.

(E) The interest of Cameron's fancy-subject pictures consists in what they tell us about the sitters and not in the imaginary scenes they portray.

9. The author mentions the props employed in *The Passing of Arthur* as

(A) examples of amateurish aspects of the work
(B) evidence of the transformative power of theater
(C) testimonies to Cameron's ingenuity
(D) indications that the work is intended ironically
(E) support for a negative appraisal of the work

10. Which one of the following, if true, would most help to explain the claim about suspension of disbelief in lines 34–36?

(A) Sitting for a painting typically takes much longer than sitting for a photograph.

(B) Paintings, unlike photographs, can depict obviously impossible situations.

(C) All of the sitters for a painting do not have to be present at the same time.

(D) A painter can suppress details about a sitter that are at odds with an imaginary persona.

(E) Paintings typically bear the stylistic imprint of an artist, school, or period.

GO ON TO THE NEXT PAGE.

11. Based on the passage, Cameron is most like which one of the following in relation to her fancy-subject pictures?

(A) a playwright who introduces incongruous elements to preserve an aesthetic distance between characters and audience

(B) a rap artist whose lyrics are designed to subvert the meaning of a song sampled in his recording

(C) a sculptor whose works possess a certain grandeur even though they are clearly constructed out of ordinary objects

(D) an architect whose buildings are designed to be as functional as possible

(E) a film director who employs ordinary people as actors in order to give the appearance of a documentary

12. Based on the passage, the author would agree with each of the following statements EXCEPT:

(A) A less realistic medium can be more conducive to suspension of disbelief than a more realistic medium.

(B) Amateurishness is a positive quality in some works of art.

(C) What might appear to be an incongruity in a narrative photograph can actually enhance its aesthetic value.

(D) We are sometimes aware of both the real and the imaginary persona of an actor in a drama.

(E) A work of art succeeds only to the extent that it realizes the artist's intentions.

13. The passage provides the most support for inferring that in Cameron's era

(A) there was little interest in photographs documenting contemporary life

(B) photography was practiced mainly by wealthy amateurs

(C) publicity stills of actors were coming into vogue

(D) there were no professional artist's models

(E) the time required to take a picture was substantial

14. The discussion of suspension of disbelief in the second paragraph serves which one of the following purposes?

(A) It is the main conclusion of the passage, for which the discussion of Cameron's fancy-subject pictures serves as a case study.

(B) It introduces a contrast the author uses in characterizing the peculiar nature of our response to Cameron's fancy-subject pictures.

(C) It is the key step in an argument supporting the author's negative appraisal of the project of narrative photography.

(D) It is used to explain a criticism of Cameron's fancy-subject pictures that the author shows to be conceptually confused.

(E) It draws a contrast between narrative painting and drama to support the author's conclusion that Cameron's fancy-subject pictures are more like the former.

15. The main purpose of the passage is

(A) to chronicle Cameron's artistic development as a photographer, which culminated in her masterpiece *The Passing of Arthur*

(B) to argue that the tension between Cameron's aims and the results she achieved in some of her works enhances the works' aesthetic value

(C) to show that Cameron's essentially theatrical vision accounts for both the strengths and the weaknesses of her photographic oeuvre

(D) to explain why Cameron's project of acquiring for photography the prestige accorded to painting was doomed to failure

(E) to defend Cameron's masterpiece *The Passing of Arthur* against its detractors by showing that it transcends the homely details of its setting

GO ON TO THE NEXT PAGE.

Some critics of advertising have assumed that the creation of false needs in consumers is the principal mechanism underlying what these critics regard as its manipulative and hegemonic power. Central to this
(5) type of critique are the writings of political theorist Herbert Marcuse, who maintained that modern people succumb to oppression by believing themselves satisfied in spite of their living in an objectively unsatisfying world. This process occurs because in
(10) mass market culture the powerful psychological techniques of advertising create "needs" that are false and whose satisfaction thus contributes, not to the genuine well-being of consumers, but rather to the profit—and thereby the disproportionate power—
(15) of corporations.

Marcuse supposed that we all have certain real needs, both physical and psychological. Advertising appropriates these needs for its own purposes, forging psychological associations between them and
(20) consumer items, e.g., between sex and perfume, thereby creating a false "need" for these items. Since the quest for fulfillment is thus displaced from its true objects to consumer items, the implicit promises of advertisements are never really fulfilled
(25) and the consumer remains at some level unsatisfied.

Unfortunately, the distinction between real and false needs upon which this critique depends is extremely problematic. If Marcusians are right, we cannot, with any assurance, separate our real needs
(30) from the alleged false needs we feel as a result of the manipulation of advertisers. For, in order to do so, it would be necessary to eliminate forces of persuasion that are so prevalent in society that they have come to inform our instinctive judgments about things.
(35) But, in fact, Marcusians make a major mistake in assuming that the majority of consumers who respond to advertising do not do so autonomously. Advertising techniques are unable to induce unwilling behavior in rational, informed adults, and regulations prohibit
(40) misinformation in advertising claims. Moreover, evidence suggests that most adults understand and recognize the techniques used and are not merely passive instruments. If there is a real need for emotional fulfillment, and if we can freely and
(45) authentically choose our means of obtaining it, then free, informed individuals may choose to obtain it through the purchase of commodities or even through the enjoyment occasionally provided by advertisements themselves. It is no doubt true that in many—perhaps
(50) even most—cases the use of an advertised product does not yield the precise sort of emotional dividend that advertisements seem to promise. This does not mean, however, that consumers do not freely and intentionally use the product as a means to another sort
(55) of fulfillment, or even that its genuine fulfillment of needs must be less than the advertisement suggests.

16. Which one of the following most accurately expresses the main point of the passage?

(A) Advertising has greater social value than Marcusians have supposed, because it is both an effective means of informing consumers and often an intrinsically entertaining medium of mass communication.

(B) Even if, as Marcusians have argued, there is a theoretical difference between real and false needs, that difference is obscured in practice by the relationship of consumers to the forces of persuasion in profit-motivated, consumer-oriented societies.

(C) Marcusian arguments regarding advertisers' creation of false needs are mistaken, because individuals are able to make autonomous decisions regarding their needs and are even able to use the elements of mass market culture to achieve genuine fulfillment.

(D) Critics of advertising typically focus on the development of false needs in the consumer and do not fully consider the ability of people to make independent choices by distinguishing their own real needs from the apparent needs that advertising induces.

(E) The problematic distinction that Marcusians have drawn between real and false needs provides an inadequate basis for their attacks on advertising, because the distinction overlooks consumers' physical and psychological needs.

17. The author states that Marcuse believed that advertisers

(A) base many of their manipulative strategies on psychological research findings

(B) appeal to people's real needs in order to create false needs

(C) are restricted to a degree by regulations prohibiting misinformation

(D) exaggerate the consumer's need for independent decision-making

(E) deny that the needs they create in people are less real than other needs

GO ON TO THE NEXT PAGE.

18. The main function of the first paragraph is to

   (A) summarize the political and economic context from which Marcusian critiques of advertising arise

   (B) outline the mechanisms by which false needs originate in mass market culture

   (C) evaluate the psychological processes by which the manipulative techniques of mass market advertising influence individuals

   (D) describe the prevailing views among contemporary critics of advertising and categorize Marcuse's theories in relation to those views

   (E) describe Marcusian views regarding mass market manipulation and indicate their role in certain criticisms of advertising

19. Which one of the following is a claim that the author attributes to Marcuse?

   (A) In modern society, advertising helps lead people to think that they are satisfied.

   (B) Modern societies differ from earlier societies in that they fail to satisfy basic physical needs.

   (C) It is impossible to draw any meaningful distinction between real and false psychological needs in modern society.

   (D) Advertising in modern society has sometimes become a tool of oppression working to the benefit of totalitarian political systems.

   (E) Advertising exploits basic human needs by deriving from them certain secondary needs which, though they become real needs, subtly work to the detriment of consumers.

20. By the term "forces of persuasion" (line 32), the author most probably refers to

   (A) intentionally dishonest claims that some theorists argue are common in advertising

   (B) innate, instinctual drives that some theorists say are fundamental to human behavior

   (C) emotional pressures that some theorists claim are exerted over individuals by society as a whole

   (D) subtle practices of social indoctrination that some theorists say are sponsored by the state

   (E) manipulative influences that some theorists say go unrecognized by those affected by them

21. Which one of the following sentences would most logically complete the passage?

   (A) Therefore, while in principle there might be grounds for holding that advertising is detrimental to society, the Marcusian critique does not provide such grounds.

   (B) Therefore, although Marcusian claims about advertising are rationally justified, the mistake of many recent critics of advertising is in their use of these claims for political gain.

   (C) Therefore, any shift in basic assumptions required to correct the abuses of advertising will require a change in the perception of human nature held by corporate leaders.

   (D) Therefore, while emphasizing only detrimental social aspects of advertising, Marcusians have failed to consider that such aspects are clearly outweighed by numerous social benefits.

   (E) Therefore, the Marcusian critique of advertising is mistaken except in its claim that advertisers exert economic power over those few people who are unable or unwilling to distinguish real from false needs.

GO ON TO THE NEXT PAGE.

Passage A

There are two principles that are fundamental to a theory of justice regarding property. The principle of justice in acquisition specifies the conditions under which someone can legitimately come to own
(5) something that was previously not owned by anyone. The principle of justice in transfer specifies the conditions under which the transfer of property from one person to another is justified.

Given such principles, if the world were wholly
(10) just, the following definition would exhaustively cover the subject of justice regarding property:

1. A person who acquires property in accordance with the principle of justice in acquisition is entitled to that property.
(15) 2. A person who acquires property in accordance with the principle of justice in transfer, from someone else who is entitled to the property, is entitled to the property.

3. No one is entitled to any property except by
(20) (repeated) applications of 1 and 2.

However, not all actual situations are generated in accordance with the principles of justice in acquisition and justice in transfer. Some people steal from others or defraud them, for example. The existence of past
(25) injustice raises the issue of the rectification of injustice. If past injustice has shaped present ownership in various ways, what, if anything, ought to be done to rectify that injustice? A principle of rectification would use historical information about previous
(30) situations and injustices done in them, and information about the actual course of events that flowed from these injustices, to produce a description of the property ownership that should have resulted. Actual ownership of property must then be brought
(35) into conformity with this description.

Passage B

In 1790, the United States Congress passed the Indian Nonintercourse Act, which requires that all transfers of lands from Native Americans to others be approved by the federal government. The law has not
(40) been changed in any relevant respect, and it remains in effect today. Its purpose is clear. It was meant to guarantee security to Native Americans against fraudulent acquisition by others of the Native Americans' land holdings. Several suits have been
(45) initiated by Native American tribes for recovery of lands held by them when the Nonintercourse Act took effect.

One natural (one might almost say obvious) way of reasoning about Native American claims to land in
(50) North America is this: Native Americans were the first human occupants of this land. Before the European invasion of North America, the land belonged to them. In the course of that invasion and its aftermath, the land was illicitly taken from them. The current owners
(55) lack a well-founded right to the land, which now lies illicitly in their hands. Ideally, the land should be restored to its rightful owners. This may be impractical; compromises might have to be made. But the original wrong can most easily be righted by returning the land
(60) to them—or by returning it wherever that is feasible.

22. Which one of the following most accurately describes the main purpose for which passage A was written and the main purpose for which passage B was written?

(A) Passage A: to propose a solution to a moral problem
Passage B: to criticize a proposed solution to a moral problem

(B) Passage A: to sketch a general outline of a branch of moral theory
Passage B: to give a particular moral analysis of a real case

(C) Passage A: to spell out the details of two fundamental principles
Passage B: to examine a case that exemplifies a moral ideal

(D) Passage A: to argue for a particular moral ideal
Passage B: to question the assumptions of a moral theory

(E) Passage A: to advocate the use of certain moral principles
Passage B: to provide a counterexample to some widely held moral principles

23. Both passages explicitly mention which one of the following?

(A) transfer of property from one owner to another
(B) a legal basis for recovery of property
(C) entitlement to property in a wholly just world
(D) practicability of rectification of past injustice
(E) injustice committed as part of an invasion

24. Which one of the following is true of the relationship between passage A and the second paragraph of passage B?

(A) The second paragraph of passage B attempts to develop a broader version of the theory presented in passage A.

(B) The second paragraph of passage B purports to state facts that bolster the argument made in passage A.

(C) The argument in the second paragraph of passage B is structurally parallel to the argument in passage A, but the subject matter of the two is different.

(D) Passage A presents a theory that tends to support the argument presented in the second paragraph of passage B.

(E) The second paragraph of passage B attempts to undermine the theory presented in passage A.

GO ON TO THE NEXT PAGE.

25. Based on what can be inferred from their titles, the relationship between which one of the following pairs of documents is most analogous to the relationship between passage A and passage B?

(A) "Card Counting for Everyone: A Can't-Lose System for Beating the Dealer"
"The Evils of Gambling"

(B) "Mayor McConnell Is Unfit to Serve"
"Why Mayor McConnell Should be Reelected"

(C) "Pruning Fruit Trees: A Guide for the Novice"
"Easy Recipes for Beginning Cooks"

(D) "Notable Failures of the STORM Weather Forecasting Model"
"Meteorologists' Best Tool Yet: The STORM Forecasting Model"

(E) "Fundamentals of Building Construction and Repair"
"Engineering Report: The Repairs Needed by the Thales Building"

26. The author of passage A would be most likely to characterize the purpose of the Indian Nonintercourse Act as which one of the following?

(A) legitimization of actual property holdings during the eighteenth century

(B) clarification of existing laws regarding transfer of property

(C) assurance of conformity to the principle of justice in acquisition

(D) prevention of violations of the principle of justice in transfer

(E) implementation of a principle of rectification

27. Which one of the following most accurately describes the difference in approach taken by passage A as compared to passage B?

(A) Passage A espouses a general view without providing details, while passage B sketches an argument that it does not necessarily endorse.

(B) Passage A argues for the superiority of one view over competing views, while passage B considers only a single view.

(C) Passage A invokes commonly held principles to support a policy recommendation, while passage B relies on the views of established authorities to support its claims.

(D) Passage A briefly states a view and then provides an argument for it, while passage B provides a detailed statement of a view but no argument.

(E) Passage A provides an argument in support of a view, while passage B attempts to undermine a view.

S T O P

IF YOU FINISH BEFORE TIME IS CALLED, YOU MAY CHECK YOUR WORK ON THIS SECTION ONLY.
DO NOT WORK ON ANY OTHER SECTION IN THE TEST.

SECTION II

Time—35 minutes

25 Questions

Directions: The questions in this section are based on the reasoning contained in brief statements or passages. For some questions, more than one of the choices could conceivably answer the question. However, you are to choose the best answer; that is, the response that most accurately and completely answers the question. You should not make assumptions that are by commonsense standards implausible, superfluous, or incompatible with the passage. After you have chosen the best answer, blacken the corresponding space on your answer sheet.

1. Editorial: The city has chosen a contractor to upgrade the heating systems in public buildings. Only 40 percent of the technicians employed by this contractor are certified by the Heating Technicians Association. So the city selected a contractor 60 percent of whose technicians are unqualified, which is an outrage.

    Which one of the following is an assumption required by the argument in the editorial?

    (A) Certified technicians receive higher pay than uncertified technicians.
    (B) There are no contractors with fewer than 40 percent of their technicians certified.
    (C) Technicians who lack certification are not qualified technicians.
    (D) Qualified technicians installed the heating systems to be upgraded.
    (E) The contractor hired by the city has personal ties to city officials.

2. Jeneta: Increasingly, I've noticed that when a salesperson thanks a customer for making a purchase, the customer also says "Thank you" instead of saying "You're welcome." I've even started doing that myself. But when a friend thanks a friend for a favor, the response is always "You're welcome."

    Which one of the following, if true, most helps to explain the discrepancy that Jeneta observes in people's responses?

    (A) Customers regard themselves as doing salespeople a favor by buying from them as opposed to someone else.
    (B) Salespeople are often instructed by their employers to thank customers, whereas customers are free to say what they want.
    (C) Salespeople do not regard customers who buy from them as doing them a favor.
    (D) The way that people respond to being thanked is generally determined by habit rather than by conscious decision.
    (E) In a commercial transaction, as opposed to a favor, the customer feels that the benefits are mutual.

3. Some video game makers have sold the movie rights for popular games. However, this move is rarely good from a business perspective. After all, StarQuanta sold the movie rights to its popular game *Nostroma*, but the poorly made film adaptation of the game was hated by critics and the public alike. Subsequent versions of the *Nostroma* video game, although better than the original, sold poorly.

    The reasoning in the argument is most vulnerable to criticism in that the argument

    (A) draws a general conclusion on the basis of just one individual case
    (B) infers that a product will be disliked by the public merely from the claim that the product was disliked by critics
    (C) restates as a conclusion a claim earlier presented as evidence for that conclusion
    (D) takes for granted that products with similar content that are in different media will be of roughly equal popularity
    (E) treats a requirement for a product to be popular as something that ensures that a product will be popular

GO ON TO THE NEXT PAGE.

4. Principle: The executive in a given company whose compensation package is determined by advice of an external consultant is likely to be overcompensated if the consultant also has business interests with the company the executive manages.

Which one of the following judgments conforms most closely to the principle stated above?

(A) The president of the Troskco Corporation is definitely overpaid, since he receives in salary and benefits almost 40 times more than the average employee of Troskco receives.

(B) The president of the Troskco Corporation is probably overpaid, since his total annual compensation package was determined five years ago, when the company's profits were at an all-time high.

(C) The president of the Troskco Corporation is probably not overpaid, since his total compensation package was determined by the Troskco board of directors without retaining the services of an external compensation consultant.

(D) The president of Troskco Corporation is probably overpaid, since the Troskco board of directors determined his compensation by following the advice of an external consultant who has many other contracts with Troskco.

(E) The president of Troskco Corporation is definitely not overpaid, since the external consultant the board of directors retained to advise on executive salaries has no other contracts with Troskco.

5. Science writer: Lemaître argued that the universe began with the explosion of a "primeval atom," a singular point of infinite gravity in space and time. If this is correct, our current observations should reveal galaxies accelerating away from one another. This is precisely what we observe. Yet because there is another theory—the oscillating universe theory—that makes exactly this same prediction, Lemaître's theory must be considered inadequate.

Which one of the following most accurately describes a flaw in the science writer's reasoning?

(A) The conclusion is derived partly from assertions attributed to a purported expert whose credibility is not established.

(B) The conclusion is based on a shift in meaning of a key term from one part of the argument to another part.

(C) The science writer takes for granted the existence of a causal connection between observed phenomena.

(D) The science writer fails to see that one theory's correctly predicting observed data cannot itself constitute evidence against an alternative theory that also does this.

(E) The science writer presumes, without providing justification, that there are only two possible explanations for the phenomena in question.

6. Critic: The criticism of the popular film comedy *Quirks* for not being realistic is misguided. It is certainly true that the characters are too stylized to be real people. That could be problematic, but in this case the resulting film is funny. And that is the important thing for a comedy.

Which one of the following principles, if valid, most helps to justify the reasoning in the critic's argument?

(A) Films should be judged on how well they accurately capture the world.

(B) Films are successful as long as they are popular.

(C) Film comedies should find their humor in their stylistic portrayals.

(D) Films are successful if they succeed within their genre.

(E) Films should try to stay entirely within a single genre.

7. Party X has recently been accused by its opposition, Party Y, of accepting international campaign contributions, which is illegal. Such accusations are, however, ill founded. Three years ago, Party Y itself was involved in a scandal in which it was discovered that its national committee seriously violated campaign laws.

Which one of the following contains flawed reasoning most similar to the flawed reasoning in the argument above?

(A) The plaintiff accuses the defendant of violating campaign laws, but the accusations are ill founded. While the defendant's actions may violate certain laws, they are not immoral, because the laws in question are unjust.

(B) The plaintiff accuses the defendant of violating campaign laws, but these accusations show the plaintiff to be hypocritical, because the plaintiff has engaged in similar conduct.

(C) The plaintiff accuses the defendant of violating campaign laws, and, in the past, courts have declared such violations illegal. Nevertheless, because the plaintiff recently engaged in actions that were similar to those of the defendant, the plaintiff's accusations are ill founded.

(D) The plaintiff accuses the defendant of violating campaign laws, but these accusations are ill founded. They are clearly an attempt to stir up controversy, because they were made just two weeks before the election.

(E) The plaintiff accuses the defendant of voting only for campaign laws that would favor the defendant's party. This accusation is ill founded, however, because it attacks the defendant's motivations instead of addressing the arguments the defendant has put forth justifying these votes.

8. Biologist: Marine animals known as box jellyfish have eyes with well-formed lenses capable of producing sharp images that reveal fine detail. But the box jellyfish's retinas are too far forward to receive a clear image, so these jellyfish can receive only a blurry image that reveals prominent features of objects but not fine detail. This example shows that eyes are adapted only to an animal's needs rather than to some abstract sense of how a good eye would be designed.

The argument requires assuming which one of the following?

(A) Box jellyfish are the only kind of jellyfish with retinas that do not focus clearly.

(B) Box jellyfish have a need to detect prominent features of objects but not fine details.

(C) Box jellyfish would benefit from having retinas that allowed their eyes to focus more sharply.

(D) Box jellyfish developed from jellyfish whose retinas received clear images.

(E) Box jellyfish use vision as their main means of detecting prey.

9. Columnist: Research shows significant reductions in the number of people smoking, and especially in the number of first-time smokers in those countries that have imposed stringent restrictions on tobacco advertising. This provides substantial grounds for disputing tobacco companies' claims that advertising has no significant causal impact on the tendency to smoke.

Which one of the following, if true, most undermines the columnist's reasoning?

(A) People who smoke are unlikely to quit merely because they are no longer exposed to tobacco advertising.

(B) Broadcast media tend to have stricter restrictions on tobacco advertising than do print media.

(C) Restrictions on tobacco advertising are imposed only in countries where a negative attitude toward tobacco use is already widespread and increasing.

(D) Most people who begin smoking during adolescence continue to smoke throughout their lives.

(E) People who are largely unaffected by tobacco advertising tend to be unaffected by other kinds of advertising as well.

GO ON TO THE NEXT PAGE.

10. Actor: Bertolt Brecht's plays are not genuinely successful dramas. The roles in Brecht's plays express such incongruous motives and beliefs that audiences, as well as the actors playing the roles, invariably find it difficult, at best, to discern any of the characters' personalities. But, for a play to succeed as a drama, audiences must care what happens to at least some of its characters.

The conclusion of the actor's argument can be properly drawn if which one of the following is assumed?

(A) An audience that cannot readily discern a character's personality will not take any interest in that character.

(B) A character's personality is determined primarily by the motives and beliefs of that character.

(C) The extent to which a play succeeds as a drama is directly proportional to the extent to which the play's audiences care about its characters.

(D) If the personalities of a play's characters are not readily discernible by the actors playing the roles, then those personalities are not readily discernible by the play's audience.

(E) All plays that, unlike Brecht's plays, have characters with whom audiences empathize succeed as dramas.

11. Municipal legislator: The mayor proposes that the city accept a lighting company's gift of several high-tech streetlights. Surely there would be no problem in accepting these despite some people's fear that the company wants to influence the city's decision regarding park lighting contracts. The only ulterior motive I can find is the company's desire to have its products seen by mayors who will visit the city for an upcoming convention. In any case, favoritism in city contracts is prevented by our competitive-bidding procedure.

Which one of the following most accurately expresses the main conclusion of the municipal legislator's argument?

(A) Some people's fear that the company wants to influence the city's decision regarding park lighting contracts is unfounded.

(B) The mayor's proposal to accept the gift of streetlights should not be considered problematic.

(C) It is not appropriate that any company should have the unique opportunity to display its products to mayors attending the upcoming convention.

(D) The city's competitive-bidding procedure prevents favoritism in the dispensing of city contracts.

(E) The lighting company's desire to display its products to visiting mayors is the real motivation behind the suggested gift of streetlights.

12. The chairperson should not have released the Election Commission's report to the public, for the chairperson did not consult any other members of the commission about releasing the report before having it released.

The argument's conclusion can be properly inferred if which one of the following is assumed?

(A) It would have been permissible for the chairperson to release the commission's report to the public only if most other members of the commission had first given their consent.

(B) All of the members of the commission had signed the report prior to its release.

(C) The chairperson would not have been justified in releasing the commission's report if any members of the commission had serious reservations about the report's content.

(D) The chairperson would have been justified in releasing the report only if each of the commission's members would have agreed to its being released had they been consulted.

(E) Some members of the commission would have preferred that the report not be released to the public.

13. Reformer: A survey of police departments keeps track of the national crime rate, which is the annual number of crimes per 100,000 people. The survey shows no significant reduction in the crime rate in the past 20 years, but the percentage of the population in prison has increased substantially, and public expenditure on prisons has grown at an alarming rate. This demonstrates that putting more people in prison cannot help to reduce crime.

A flaw in the reformer's argument is that it

(A) infers without justification that because the national crime rate has increased, the number of crimes reported by each police department has increased

(B) ignores the possibility that the crime rate would have significantly increased if it had not been for the greater rate of imprisonment

(C) overlooks the possibility that the population has increased significantly over the past 20 years

(D) presumes, without providing warrant, that alternative measures for reducing crime would be more effective than imprisonment

(E) takes for granted that the number of prisoners must be proportional to the number of crimes committed

GO ON TO THE NEXT PAGE.

14. Inez: Space-exploration programs pay for themselves many times over, since such programs result in technological advances with everyday, practical applications. Space exploration is more than the search for knowledge for its own sake; investment in space exploration is such a productive investment in developing widely useful technology that we can't afford not to invest in space exploration.

Winona: It is absurd to try to justify funding for space exploration merely by pointing out that such programs will lead to technological advances. If technology with practical applications is all that is desired, then it should be funded directly.

Winona responds to Inez by

(A) showing that there is no evidence that the outcome Inez anticipates will in fact be realized

(B) suggesting that Inez has overlooked evidence that directly argues against the programs Inez supports

(C) demonstrating that the pieces of evidence that Inez cites contradict each other

(D) providing evidence that the beneficial effects that Inez desires can be achieved only at great expense

(E) claiming that a goal that Inez mentions could be pursued without the programs Inez endorses

15. Marketing consultant: Last year I predicted that LRG's latest advertising campaign would be unpopular with customers and ineffective in promoting new products. But LRG ignored my predictions and took the advice of a competing consultant. This season's sales figures show that sales are down and LRG's new products are selling especially poorly. Thus, the advertising campaign was ill conceived.

The marketing consultant's reasoning is most vulnerable to criticism on the grounds that

(A) it takes for granted that LRG's sales would not have been lower still in the absence of the competitor's advertising campaign

(B) it fails to consider that economic factors unrelated to the advertising campaign may have caused LRG's low sales figures

(C) it takes for granted that in LRG's industry, new products should outsell established products

(D) it takes for granted that the higher sales of established products are due to effective advertising

(E) it confuses a condition necessary for increasing product sales with a condition that will ensure increased sales

16. The top prize in architecture, the Pritzker Prize, is awarded for individual achievement, like Nobel Prizes for science. But architects are judged by their buildings, and buildings are the result of teamwork. As achievements, buildings are not like scientific discoveries, but like movies, which compete for awards for best picture. Thus, it would be better if the top prize in architecture were awarded to the best building rather than the best architect.

The argument proceeds by

(A) reaching a conclusion about the way something should be done in one field on the basis of comparisons with corresponding practices in other fields

(B) making a distinction between two different types of objects in order to conclude that one has more inherent value than the other

(C) pointing to similarities between two practices as a basis for concluding that criticisms of one practice can rightly be applied to the other

(D) arguing that because two different fields are disanalogous, the characteristics of one field are not relevant to justifying a conclusion about the other

(E) contending that an action is inappropriate by presenting an argument that a corresponding action in an analogous case is inappropriate

GO ON TO THE NEXT PAGE.

17. If Suarez is not the most qualified of the candidates for sheriff, then Anderson is. Thus, if the most qualified candidate is elected and Suarez is not elected, then Anderson will be.

The reasoning in which one of the following is most similar to the reasoning in the argument above?

(A)   If the excavation contract does not go to the lowest bidder, then it will go to Caldwell. So if Qiu gets the contract and Caldwell does not, then the contract will have been awarded to the lowest bidder.

(B)   If the lowest bidder on the sanitation contract is not Dillon, then it is Ramsey. So if the contract goes to the lowest bidder and it does not go to Dillon, then it will go to Ramsey.

(C)   If Kapshaw is not awarded the landscaping contract, then Johnson will be. So if the contract goes to the lowest bidder and it does not go to Johnson, then it will go to Kapshaw.

(D)   If Holihan did not submit the lowest bid on the maintenance contract, then neither did Easton. So if the contract goes to the lowest bidder and it does not go to Easton, then it will not go to Holihan either.

(E)   If Perez is not the lowest bidder on the catering contract, then Sullivan is. So if Sullivan does not get the contract and Perez does not get it either, then it will not be awarded to the lowest bidder.

18. Critic: An art historian argues that because fifteenth-century European paintings were generally more planimetric (that is, two-dimensional with no attempt at suggesting depth) than were sixteenth-century paintings, fifteenth-century painters had a greater mastery of painting than did sixteenth-century painters. However, this conclusion is wrong. Fifteenth-century European painters did not have a greater mastery of painting, for the degree to which a painting is planimetric is irrelevant to the painter's mastery.

The argument is flawed in that it

(A)   rejects a position merely because the proponent of the position has other objectionable views

(B)   illicitly relies on two different meanings of the term "mastery"

(C)   takes a necessary condition for an argument's being inadequate to be a sufficient condition for an argument's being inadequate

(D)   bases its conclusion on two claims that contradict each other

(E)   rejects a position on the grounds that an inadequate argument has been made for it

19. A carved flint object depicting a stylized human head with an open mouth was found in a Stone Age tomb in Ireland. Some archaeologists believe that the object was a weapon—the head of a warrior's mace—but it is too small for that purpose. Because of its size and the fact that an open mouth symbolizes speaking, the object was probably the head of a speaking staff, a communal object passed around a small assembly to indicate who has the right to speak.

Which one of the following, if true, would most weaken the argument?

(A)   The tomb in which the object was found did not contain any other objects that might have been weapons.

(B)   Communal objects were normally passed from one generation to the next in Stone Age Ireland.

(C)   The object was carved with an artistry that was rare in Stone Age Ireland.

(D)   The tomb in which the object was found was that of a politically prominent person.

(E)   A speaking staff with a stone head is thought to symbolize a warrior's mace.

20. The advent of chemical fertilizers led the farmers in a certain region to abandon the practice of periodically growing a "green-manure" crop, such as alfalfa, in a field to rejuvenate its soil. As a result, the soil structure in a typical farm field in the region is poor. So to significantly improve the soil structure, farmers will need to abandon the use of chemical fertilizers.

The argument relies on the assumption that

(A)   most, if not all, farmers in the region who abandon the use of chemical fertilizers will periodically grow alfalfa

(B)   applying chemical fertilizers to green-manure crops, such as alfalfa, has no positive effect on their growth

(C)   the most important factor influencing the soil quality of a farm field is soil structure

(D)   chemical fertilizers themselves have a destructive effect on the soil structure of farm fields

(E)   many, if not all, farmers in the region will not grow green-manure crops unless they abandon the use of chemical fertilizers

GO ON TO THE NEXT PAGE.

21. Most of the students who took Spanish 101 at the university last semester attended every class session. However, each student who received a grade lower than B minus missed at least one class session.

Which one of the following statements about the students who took Spanish 101 at the university last semester can be properly inferred from the information above?

(A) At least some of the students who received a grade of A minus or higher attended every class session.

(B) Most, if not all, of the students who missed at least one class session received a grade lower than B minus.

(C) Most of the students received a grade higher than B minus.

(D) At least one student who received a grade of B minus or higher missed one or more class sessions.

(E) More than half of the students received a grade of B minus or higher.

22. Because the native salmon in Lake Clearwater had nearly disappeared, sockeye salmon were introduced in 1940. After being introduced, this genetically uniform group of sockeyes split into two distinct populations that do not interbreed, one inhabiting deep areas of the lake and the other inhabiting shallow areas. Since the two populations now differ genetically, some researchers hypothesize that each has adapted genetically to its distinct habitat.

Which of the following, if true, most strongly supports the researchers' hypothesis?

(A) Neither of the two populations of sockeyes has interbred with the native salmon.

(B) When the native salmon in Lake Clearwater were numerous, they comprised two distinct populations that did not interbreed.

(C) Most types of salmon that inhabit lakes spend part of the time in shallow water and part in deeper water.

(D) One of the populations of sockeyes is virtually identical genetically to the sockeyes originally introduced in 1940.

(E) The total number of sockeye salmon in the lake is not as large as the number of native salmon had been many years ago.

23. A developing country can substantially increase its economic growth if its businesspeople are willing to invest in modern industries that have not yet been pursued there. But being the first to invest in an industry is very risky. Moreover, businesspeople have little incentive to take this risk since if the business succeeds, many other people will invest in the same industry, and the competition will cut into their profits.

The statements above, if true, most strongly support which one of the following claims?

(A) Once a developing country has at least one business in a modern industry, further investment in that industry will not contribute to the country's economic growth.

(B) In developing countries, there is greater competition within modern industries than within traditional industries.

(C) A developing country can increase its prospects for economic growth by providing added incentive for investment in modern industries that have not yet been pursued there.

(D) A developing country will not experience economic growth unless its businesspeople invest in modern industries.

(E) Investments in a modern industry in a developing country carry little risk as long as the country has at least one other business in that industry.

GO ON TO THE NEXT PAGE.

24. A survey of a city's concertgoers found that almost all of them were dissatisfied with the local concert hall. A large majority of them expressed a strong preference for wider seats and better acoustics. And, even though the survey respondents were told that the existing concert hall cannot feasibly be modified to provide these features, most of them opposed the idea of tearing down the existing structure and replacing it with a concert hall with wider seats and better acoustics.

Which one of the following, if true, most helps to explain the apparent conflict in the concertgoers' views, as revealed by the survey?

(A) Before any of the survey questions were asked, the respondents were informed that the survey was sponsored by a group that advocates replacing the existing concert hall.

(B) Most of the people who live in the vicinity of the existing concert hall do not want it to be torn down.

(C) The city's construction industry will receive more economic benefit from the construction of a new concert hall than from renovations to the existing concert hall.

(D) A well-publicized plan is being considered by the city government that would convert the existing concert hall into a public auditorium and build a new concert hall nearby.

(E) Many popular singers and musicians who currently do not hold concerts in the city would begin to hold concerts there if a new concert hall were built.

25. Student: Before completing my research paper, I want to find the book from which I copied a passage to quote in the paper. Without the book, I will be unable to write an accurate citation, and without an accurate citation, I will be unable to include the quotation. Hence, since the completed paper will be much better with the quotation than without, _____.

Which one of the following most logically completes the student's argument?

(A) I will have to include an inaccurate citation

(B) I will be unable to complete my research paper

(C) if I do not find the book, my research paper will suffer

(D) if I do not find the book, I will include the quotation without an accurate citation

(E) if I do not find the book, I will be unable to complete my research paper

S T O P

IF YOU FINISH BEFORE TIME IS CALLED, YOU MAY CHECK YOUR WORK ON THIS SECTION ONLY. DO NOT WORK ON ANY OTHER SECTION IN THE TEST.

SECTION III

Time—35 minutes

23 Questions

Directions: Each group of questions in this section is based on a set of conditions. In answering some of the questions, it may be useful to draw a rough diagram. Choose the response that most accurately and completely answers each question and blacken the corresponding space on your answer sheet.

Questions 1–7

A record producer is planning the contents of a CD consisting of a sequence of exactly five instrumental pieces—*Reciprocity, Salammbo, Trapezoid, Vancouver,* and *Wisteria*. To create and sustain certain moods, the sequence of pieces will satisfy the following constraints:

Salammbo must be earlier than *Vancouver*.

Trapezoid must either be earlier than both *Reciprocity* and *Salammbo* or later than both *Reciprocity* and *Salammbo*.

Wisteria must either be earlier than both *Reciprocity* and *Trapezoid* or later than both *Reciprocity* and *Trapezoid*.

1. The five pieces could appear in which one of the following sequences on the CD, in order from first to last?

(A) *Reciprocity, Trapezoid, Wisteria, Salammbo, Vancouver*

(B) *Salammbo, Reciprocity, Trapezoid, Vancouver, Wisteria*

(C) *Trapezoid, Wisteria, Salammbo, Vancouver, Reciprocity*

(D) *Vancouver, Wisteria, Salammbo, Reciprocity, Trapezoid*

(E) *Wisteria, Salammbo, Vancouver, Trapezoid, Reciprocity*

GO ON TO THE NEXT PAGE.

2. If *Salammbo* is the fourth piece on the CD, then which one of the following must be true?

    (A)   *Reciprocity* is earlier on the CD than *Wisteria*.
    (B)   *Salammbo* is earlier on the CD than *Trapezoid*.
    (C)   *Trapezoid* is earlier on the CD than *Reciprocity*.
    (D)   *Vancouver* is earlier on the CD than *Wisteria*.
    (E)   *Wisteria* is earlier on the CD than *Trapezoid*.

3. If *Reciprocity* is the first piece on the CD, then which one of the following could be true?

    (A)   *Trapezoid* is the second piece on the CD.
    (B)   *Vancouver* is the third piece on the CD.
    (C)   *Wisteria* is the third piece on the CD.
    (D)   *Salammbo* is the fourth piece on the CD.
    (E)   *Trapezoid* is the last piece on the CD.

4. If *Trapezoid* is the second piece on the CD, then which one of the following could be true?

    (A)   *Salammbo* is the first piece on the CD.
    (B)   *Reciprocity* is the first piece on the CD.
    (C)   *Vancouver* is the third piece on the CD.
    (D)   *Wisteria* is the fourth piece on the CD.
    (E)   *Reciprocity* is the last piece on the CD.

5. The first and second pieces on the CD, listed in order, could be

    (A)   *Reciprocity* and *Vancouver*
    (B)   *Reciprocity* and *Wisteria*
    (C)   *Salammbo* and *Trapezoid*
    (D)   *Trapezoid* and *Wisteria*
    (E)   *Wisteria* and *Salammbo*

6. If *Vancouver* is the second piece on the CD, then which one of the following could be true?

    (A)   *Wisteria* is the first piece on the CD.
    (B)   *Salammbo* is the third piece on the CD.
    (C)   *Trapezoid* is the third piece on the CD.
    (D)   *Reciprocity* is the fourth piece on the CD.
    (E)   *Reciprocity* is the last piece on the CD.

7. If *Wisteria* is the first piece on the CD, then which one of the following CANNOT be true?

    (A)   *Trapezoid* is the third piece on the CD.
    (B)   *Vancouver* is the third piece on the CD.
    (C)   *Salammbo* is the fourth piece on the CD.
    (D)   *Vancouver* is the fourth piece on the CD.
    (E)   *Trapezoid* is the last piece on the CD.

GO ON TO THE NEXT PAGE.

Questions 8–13

At a business symposium there will be exactly five speakers: Long, Molina, Xiao, Yoshida, and Zimmerman. Each speaker will give exactly one speech, in either the Gold Room or the Rose Room. In each room, there will be exactly one speech at 1 P.M. and one speech at 2 P.M. In one of the rooms, yet to be determined, there will also be a speech at 3 P.M. The schedule of speeches is constrained by the following:

Molina's speech must be earlier than Long's, and in the same room.

Neither Xiao's speech nor Yoshida's speech can be earlier than Zimmerman's.

If Long's speech is in the Gold Room, then Xiao's and Zimmerman's speeches must both be in the Rose Room.

8. Which one of the following could be the speeches given in each room, listed in the order in which they occur?

(A)   Gold Room: Molina's, Long's
      Rose Room: Zimmerman's, Xiao's, Yoshida's

(B)   Gold Room: Molina's, Yoshida's, Long's
      Rose Room: Xiao's, Zimmerman's

(C)   Gold Room: Xiao's, Molina's, Long's
      Rose Room: Zimmerman's, Yoshida's

(D)   Gold Room: Yoshida's, Long's, Molina's
      Rose Room: Zimmerman's, Xiao's

(E)   Gold Room: Zimmerman's, Molina's
      Rose Room: Xiao's, Yoshida's, Long's

GO ON TO THE NEXT PAGE.

9. Which one of the following pairs of speeches CANNOT be given at the same time?

   (A)   Long's and Yoshida's
   (B)   Long's and Zimmerman's
   (C)   Molina's and Xiao's
   (D)   Xiao's and Yoshida's
   (E)   Yoshida's and Zimmerman's

10. If Xiao's speech is at 3 P.M., which one of the following CANNOT be true?

   (A)   Long's speech is in the same room as Yoshida's.
   (B)   Molina's speech is in the same room as Xiao's.
   (C)   Xiao's speech is in the same room as Yoshida's.
   (D)   Xiao's speech is in the same room as Zimmerman's.
   (E)   Yoshida's speech is in the same room as Zimmerman's.

11. Which one of the following could be a complete and accurate list of the speeches given in the Gold Room, in the order in which they occur?

   (A)   Long's, Molina's
   (B)   Molina's, Yoshida's
   (C)   Molina's, Yoshida's, Long's
   (D)   Yoshida's, Zimmerman's, Xiao's
   (E)   Zimmerman's, Molina's, Long's

12. If Yoshida's speech is at 1 P.M., which one of the following could be true?

   (A)   Long's speech is at 1 P.M. in the Gold Room.
   (B)   Long's speech is at 2 P.M. in the Rose Room.
   (C)   Molina's speech is at 2 P.M. in the Gold Room.
   (D)   Xiao's speech is at 3 P.M. in the Gold Room.
   (E)   Xiao's speech is at 1 P.M. in the Rose Room.

13. Which one of the following, if substituted for the constraint that neither Xiao's speech nor Yoshida's speech can be earlier than Zimmerman's, would have the same effect in determining the schedule of speeches with regard to rooms and times?

   (A)   Long's speech must be at 3 P.M.
   (B)   Molina's speech cannot be earlier than Zimmerman's.
   (C)   Either Xiao's speech or Yoshida's speech must be after Zimmerman's.
   (D)   Either Xiao's speech or Yoshida's speech or both must be at 2 P.M.
   (E)   Zimmerman's speech must be at 1 P.M.

GO ON TO THE NEXT PAGE.

Questions 14–18

During the seventeenth century, three families—the Trents, the Williamses, and the Yandells—owned the five buildings that constituted the center of their village—the forge, the granary, the inn, the mill, and the stable. Each family owned at least one of the buildings and each building was owned by exactly one of the families. The historical evidence establishes the following about the ownership of the buildings:

The Williamses owned more of the buildings than the Yandells owned.

Neither the inn nor the mill belonged to the owner of the forge.

Either the Trents owned the stable or the Yandells owned the inn, or both.

14. Which one of the following could be an accurate matching of each family to the building or buildings it owned?

(A)   Trents: the granary, the stable
        Williamses: the inn, the mill
        Yandells: the forge

(B)   Trents: the granary, the mill
        Williamses: the inn, the stable
        Yandells: the forge

(C)   Trents: the forge, the mill
        Williamses: the granary, the stable
        Yandells: the inn

(D)   Trents: the forge, the granary
        Williamses: the mill
        Yandells: the inn, the stable

(E)   Trents: the stable
        Williamses: the inn, the mill
        Yandells: the forge, the granary

GO ON TO THE NEXT PAGE.

15. Which one of the following is a pair of buildings that CANNOT both have been owned by the Trents?

 (A) the forge, the granary
 (B) the granary, the mill
 (C) the granary, the stable
 (D) the inn, the mill
 (E) the inn, the stable

16. If the Yandells owned the mill, which one of the following must be true?

 (A) The Trents owned the forge.
 (B) The Trents owned the inn.
 (C) The Williamses owned the forge.
 (D) The Williamses owned the granary.
 (E) The Williamses owned the inn.

17. If one of the families owned both the granary and the inn, which one of the following could be true?

 (A) The Trents owned the granary.
 (B) The Trents owned the mill.
 (C) The Williamses owned the forge.
 (D) The Williamses owned the stable.
 (E) The Yandells owned the inn.

18. If the Trents owned exactly one of the buildings, which one of the following is a complete and accurate list of the buildings any one of which could be the building that the Trents owned?

 (A) the forge
 (B) the forge, the mill
 (C) the inn, the stable
 (D) the forge, the granary, the mill
 (E) the forge, the mill, the stable

GO ON TO THE NEXT PAGE.

Questions 19–23

A florist is filling a customer's order for three bouquets—bouquet 1, bouquet 2, and bouquet 3. Each of the bouquets is to be composed of one or more of five kinds of flowers—lilies, peonies, roses, snapdragons, and tulips—subject to the following conditions:

Bouquets 1 and 3 cannot have any kind of flower in common.

Bouquets 2 and 3 must have exactly two kinds of flowers in common.

Bouquet 3 must have snapdragons.

If a bouquet has lilies, that bouquet must also have roses but cannot have snapdragons.

If a bouquet has tulips, that bouquet must also have peonies.

19. Which one of the following could be a complete and accurate list of the kinds of flowers in each of the bouquets?

(A)   bouquet 1: lilies, roses
        bouquet 2: peonies, roses, tulips
        bouquet 3: peonies, snapdragons, tulips

(B)   bouquet 1: peonies, roses
        bouquet 2: peonies, snapdragons
        bouquet 3: peonies, snapdragons, tulips

(C)   bouquet 1: peonies, tulips
        bouquet 2: roses, snapdragons, tulips
        bouquet 3: roses, snapdragons

(D)   bouquet 1: roses
        bouquet 2: peonies, snapdragons
        bouquet 3: lilies, peonies, snapdragons

(E)   bouquet 1: snapdragons
        bouquet 2: lilies, roses
        bouquet 3: lilies, roses

GO ON TO THE NEXT PAGE.

20. If lilies are in bouquet 1, which one of the following must be true?

   (A)   Lilies are in bouquet 2.
   (B)   Peonies are in bouquet 3.
   (C)   Roses are in bouquet 2.
   (D)   Tulips are in bouquet 2.
   (E)   Tulips are in bouquet 3.

21. If tulips are in bouquet 1, which one of the following could be a complete and accurate list of the kinds of flowers in bouquet 2?

   (A)   peonies, tulips
   (B)   peonies, snapdragons
   (C)   peonies, snapdragons, tulips
   (D)   peonies, roses, tulips
   (E)   peonies, roses, snapdragons, tulips

22. Which one of the following CANNOT be a complete and accurate list of the kinds of flowers in bouquet 2?

   (A)   lilies, roses
   (B)   peonies, tulips
   (C)   peonies, roses, snapdragons
   (D)   peonies, roses, tulips
   (E)   peonies, roses, snapdragons, tulips

23. Which one of the following CANNOT be true?

   (A)   Lilies and roses are the only kinds of flowers in bouquet 1.
   (B)   Peonies and tulips are the only kinds of flowers in bouquet 1.
   (C)   Lilies, peonies, and roses are the only kinds of flowers in bouquet 2.
   (D)   Peonies, roses, and snapdragons are the only kinds of flowers in bouquet 2.
   (E)   Peonies, snapdragons, and tulips are the only kinds of flowers in bouquet 3.

S T O P

IF YOU FINISH BEFORE TIME IS CALLED, YOU MAY CHECK YOUR WORK ON THIS SECTION ONLY.
DO NOT WORK ON ANY OTHER SECTION IN THE TEST.

SECTION IV

Time—35 minutes

26 Questions

Directions: The questions in this section are based on the reasoning contained in brief statements or passages. For some questions, more than one of the choices could conceivably answer the question. However, you are to choose the best answer; that is, the response that most accurately and completely answers the question. You should not make assumptions that are by commonsense standards implausible, superfluous, or incompatible with the passage. After you have chosen the best answer, blacken the corresponding space on your answer sheet.

1. In an experiment, ten people were asked to taste samples of coffee and rank them. Five of the people were given chocolate with the coffee, and this group subsequently reported that all the coffee samples tasted pretty much the same as one another. Five others tasted coffee only, and they were able to detect differences. Clearly, then, chocolate interferes with one's ability to taste coffee.

    Which one of the following, if true, most undermines the conclusion drawn above?

    (A)   The ten people were randomly assigned to either the group that tasted only coffee or the group that was also given chocolate, although some people had asked to be in the group that received chocolate.

    (B)   Similar results were achieved when the experiment was repeated with a different, larger group of people.

    (C)   Chocolate is normally consumed as a solid, whereas coffee is normally consumed as a liquid.

    (D)   The five people who were originally given chocolate were asked a week later to taste coffee samples without chocolate, and they still detected no differences between the coffee samples.

    (E)   Some subjects who tasted just coffee reported only subtle differences between the coffee samples, while others thought the differences were considerable.

2. Residents of a coastal community are resisting the efforts of one family to build a large house on the family's land. Although the house would not violate any town codes, the land in question is depicted in a painting by a famous and beloved landscape painter who recently died. Residents argue that the house would alter the pristine landscape and hence damage the community's artistic and historic heritage.

    Which one of the following principles, if valid, most helps to justify the reasoning of the residents opposed to building the house?

    (A)   Every possible effort should be made to preserve historic buildings that are well known and well loved.

    (B)   Communities that seek to preserve undeveloped areas of landscape or historic neighborhoods should purchase those properties for the public trust.

    (C)   Artists who choose to represent actual landscapes in their paintings have the right to demand that the owners of the land represented do not significantly alter the landscape.

    (D)   The right to build on one's own property is constrained by the artistic and historical interests of the community at large.

    (E)   In historic communities, the building and zoning regulations should prohibit construction that obstructs access to historic sites.

GO ON TO THE NEXT PAGE.

3. Moore: Sunscreen lotions, which are designed to block skin-cancer-causing ultraviolet radiation, do not do so effectively. Many scientific studies have shown that people who have consistently used these lotions develop, on average, as many skin cancers as those who have rarely, if ever, used them.

The reasoning in Moore's argument is most vulnerable to criticism on the grounds that the argument

(A) takes for granted that there are no other possible health benefits of using sunscreen lotions other than blocking skin-cancer-causing ultraviolet radiation

(B) fails to distinguish between the relative number of cases of skin cancer and the severity of those cases in measuring effectiveness at skin cancer prevention

(C) fails to consider the effectiveness of sunscreen lotions that are not specifically designed to block skin-cancer-causing ultraviolet radiation

(D) relies on evidence regarding the probability of people in different groups developing cancer that, in principle, would be impossible to challenge

(E) overlooks the possibility that people who consistently use sunscreen lotions spend more time in the sun, on average, than people who do not

4. Psychologist: Some have argued that Freudian psychotherapy is the most effective kind because it is so difficult and time consuming. But surely this does not follow. Similar reasoning—e.g., concluding that a car-repair chain has the most effective technique for repairing cars because the cars it services receive so much work and spend so much time in the shop—would never be accepted.

The reasoning technique employed by the psychologist is that of attempting to undermine an argument by

(A) introducing a principle that contradicts the one on which the argument is based

(B) questioning the truth of its premises

(C) presenting an analogous argument whose conclusion is thought to be obviously false

(D) claiming that the argument is based on a false analogy

(E) suggesting that a supposed cause of a phenomenon is actually an effect of that phenomenon

5. While biodiversity is indispensable to the survival of life on Earth, biodiversity does not require the survival of every currently existing species. For there to be life on Earth, various ecological niches must be filled; many niches, however, can be filled by more than one species.

Which one of the following statements most accurately expresses the conclusion drawn in the argument?

(A) Biodiversity does not require that all existing species continue to exist.

(B) There are various ecological niches that must be filled if there is to be life on Earth.

(C) The survival of life on Earth depends upon biodiversity.

(D) There are many ecological niches that can be filled by more than one species.

(E) The species most indispensable for biodiversity fill more than one ecological niche.

6. Clinician: Patients with immune system disorders are usually treated with a class of drugs that, unfortunately, increase the patient's risk of developing osteoporosis, a bone-loss disease. So these patients take another drug that helps to preserve existing bone. Since a drug that enhances the growth of new bone cells has now become available, these patients should take this new drug in addition to the drug that helps to preserve existing bone.

Which one of the following would be most useful to know in order to evaluate the clinician's argument?

(A) How large is the class of drugs that increase the risk of developing osteoporosis?

(B) Why are immune system disorders treated with drugs that increase the risk of developing osteoporosis?

(C) Is the new drug more expensive than the drug that helps to preserve existing bone?

(D) How long has the drug that helps to preserve existing bone been in use?

(E) To what extent does the new drug retain its efficacy when used in combination with the other drugs?

GO ON TO THE NEXT PAGE.

7. Critic: The perennial image of the "city on a hill" associates elevated locations with elevated purposes. The city's concert hall—its newest civic building—is located on a spectacular hilltop site. But because it is far from the center of the city, it cannot fulfill the purpose of a civic building. An example of a successful civic building is the art museum, which is situated in a densely populated downtown area. It encourages social cohesion and makes the city more alive.

The critic's reasoning most closely conforms to which one of the following principles?

(A) A civic building that is located in a downtown area should, if possible, be located on an elevated site.

(B) A city needs to have civic buildings if it is to have social cohesion.

(C) A civic building with an elevated purpose should be located on a spectacular site.

(D) The downtown area of a city should be designed in a way that complements the area's civic buildings.

(E) The purpose of a civic building is to encourage social cohesion and to make a city more alive.

8. Fluoride enters a region's groundwater when rain dissolves fluoride-bearing minerals in the soil. In a recent study, researchers found that when rainfall, concentrations of fluoride-bearing minerals, and other relevant variables are held constant, fluoride concentrations in groundwater are significantly higher in areas where the groundwater also contains a high concentration of sodium.

Which one of the following can most reasonably be concluded on the basis of the researchers' findings?

(A) Fluoride-bearing minerals are not the primary source of fluoride found in groundwater.

(B) Rainfall does not affect fluoride concentrations in groundwater.

(C) Sodium-bearing minerals dissolve at a faster rate than fluoride-bearing minerals.

(D) Sodium in groundwater increases the rate at which fluoride-bearing minerals dissolve.

(E) Soil that contains high concentrations of sodium-bearing minerals also contains high concentrations of fluoride-bearing minerals.

9. Fraenger's assertion that the artist Hieronymus Bosch belonged to the Brethren of the Free Spirit, a nonmainstream religious group, is unlikely to be correct. Fraenger's hypothesis explains much of Bosch's unusual subject matter. However, there is evidence that Bosch was a member of a mainstream church, and no evidence that he was a member of the Brethren.

The statement that there is no evidence that Bosch was a member of the Brethren figures in the argument in which one of the following ways?

(A) It is a premise that, when combined with the other premises, guarantees the falsity of Fraenger's assertion.

(B) It is used to support the claim that Bosch was a member of a mainstream church.

(C) It is used to dispute Fraenger's hypothesis by questioning Fraenger's credibility.

(D) It is intended to cast doubt on Fraenger's hypothesis by questioning the sufficiency of Fraenger's evidence.

(E) It is intended to help show that Bosch's choice of subject matter remains unexplained.

10. Vacuum cleaner salesperson: To prove that this Super XL vacuum cleaner is better than your old vacuum cleaner, I ran your old vacuum once over this dirty carpet. Then I ran the Super XL over the same area. All that dirt that the Super XL picked up is dirt your old vacuum left behind, proving the Super XL is the better vacuum.

The vacuum cleaner salesperson's argument is most vulnerable to the criticism that it

(A) ignores the possibility that dirt remained in the carpet even after the Super XL had been used in the test

(B) takes for granted that the Super XL will still perform better than the old vacuum cleaner when it is the same age as the old vacuum cleaner

(C) takes for granted that because the Super XL outperforms one vacuum cleaner it is the best vacuum cleaner available

(D) ignores the possibility that the amount of dirt removed in the test by the old vacuum cleaner is greater than the amount of dirt removed by the Super XL

(E) ignores the possibility that if the Super XL had been used first it would have left behind just as much dirt as did the old vacuum cleaner

GO ON TO THE NEXT PAGE.

11. Manager: This company's supply chain will develop significant weaknesses unless we make changes to our vendor contracts now. Some will argue that this problem is so far in the future that there is no need to address it today. But that is an irresponsible approach. Just imagine if a financial planner offered the same counsel to a 30-year-old client: "Don't worry, Jane, retirement is 35 years away; you don't need to save anything now." That planner would be guilty of gross malpractice.

Which one of the following most accurately expresses the overall conclusion drawn in the manager's argument?

(A) Some people argue that the supply-chain problem is so far in the future that there is no need to address it now.

(B) It would be irresponsible to postpone changes to the vendor contracts just because the supply chain will not develop weaknesses for a long time.

(C) If no changes are made to the vendor contracts, the supply chain will eventually develop significant weaknesses.

(D) In planning to meet its future obligations, a company should follow the same practices that are appropriate for an individual who is planning for retirement.

(E) Financial planners should advise their clients to save money for retirement only if retirement is many years away.

12. Worldwide, more books were sold last year than in any previous year. In particular, there were more cookbooks sold. For the first time ever, most of the cookbooks sold were not intended for beginners. Indeed, more cookbooks than ever were purchased by professional cooks. However, one of the few books available on every continent is a cookbook written for beginners, entitled *Problem-Free Cooking*.

Which one of the following is most strongly supported by the information above?

(A) Last year there were more cookbooks sold that were not intended for beginners than in any previous year.

(B) The best-selling cookbook last year was a cookbook that was intended for beginners.

(C) Sales of cookbooks intended for beginners were lower last year than in previous years.

(D) Most of the cookbooks purchased last year that were not intended for beginners were purchased by professional cooks.

(E) *Problem-Free Cooking* sold more copies last year than did any cookbook written for professional cooks.

13. In early 2003, scientists detected methane in the atmosphere of Mars. Methane is a fragile compound that falls apart when hit by the ultraviolet radiation in sunlight. So any methane in the Martian atmosphere must have been released into the atmosphere relatively recently.

The argument relies on the assumption that

(A) Mars had no methane in its atmosphere prior to 2003

(B) all methane in the Martian atmosphere is eventually exposed to sunlight

(C) methane cannot be detected until it has started to fall apart

(D) the methane that the scientists detected had been exposed to ultraviolet radiation

(E) methane in Earth's atmosphere does not fall apart as a result of exposure to ultraviolet radiation

14. Environmentalist: Pollution from gasoline burned by cars contributes to serious environmental problems. But the cost of these problems is not reflected in gasoline prices, and hence usually does not affect consumers' decisions about how much to drive. Heavier taxes on gasoline, however, would reflect this cost, and as a result consumers would pollute less.

The environmentalist's statements, if true, most strongly support which one of the following?

(A) The cost of pollution from driving should not be reflected in the price of gasoline unless the amount of pollution produced would be reduced as a result.

(B) Heavier taxes on gasoline would increase consumers' awareness of the kinds of environmental problems to which pollution from driving contributes.

(C) Consumers would purchase less gasoline, on average, if the cost of the environmental problems to which pollution from driving contributes were fully reflected in the price of gasoline.

(D) The only cost considered by most consumers when they are deciding how much to drive is the cost of gasoline.

(E) Pollution from gasoline burned by cars will be reduced only if consumers give more consideration to the cost of that pollution when deciding how much to drive.

GO ON TO THE NEXT PAGE.

15. Hine's emerald dragonflies are an endangered species that live in wetlands. The larvae of these dragonflies can survive only in the water, where they are subject to predation by several species including red devil crayfish. Surprisingly, the dragonfly populations are more likely to remain healthy in areas where red devil crayfish are present than in areas without red devil crayfish.

Which one of the following, if true, most helps to explain the surprising fact?

(A) Red devil crayfish dig chambers that remain filled with water even when the surrounding wetlands dry up.

(B) Red devil crayfish present no threat to adult Hine's emerald dragonflies.

(C) The varied diet of the red devil crayfish does not include any animal species that prey on dragonfly larvae.

(D) Red devil crayfish are found in many more locations than Hine's emerald dragonflies are.

(E) Populations of red devil crayfish in a wetland do not drop significantly if the local population of Hine's emerald dragonflies dies out.

16. Stress is a common cause of high blood pressure. By calming their minds and thereby reducing stress, some people can lower their blood pressure. And most people can calm their minds, in turn, by engaging in exercise.

Which one of the following is most strongly supported by the information above?

(A) For at least some people, having lower blood pressure has at least some tendency to cause their stress levels to be reduced.

(B) Most people with high blood pressure can lower their blood pressure by reducing their stress levels.

(C) Most people who do not exercise regularly have higher stress levels as a result.

(D) Engaging in exercise can directly lower one's blood pressure.

(E) For at least some people, engaging in exercise can cause their stress levels to be reduced.

17. A positive correlation has been found between the amount of soot in the atmosphere of cities and the frequency of a certain ailment among those cities' populations. However, the soot itself probably does not cause this ailment, since in cities where there are large amounts of soot in the air, there are usually also high concentrations of many other air pollutants.

Which one of the following statements, if true, most weakens the argument?

(A) In cities where there are high concentrations of many air pollutants but little if any soot in the air, the frequency of the ailment is just as high, on average, as it is in cities where there are large amounts of soot in the air.

(B) If the ailment rarely occurs except in cities in which there are large amounts of soot in the air, then the soot is probably the cause of the ailment.

(C) In each of the cities where there are large amounts of soot in the air but little other air pollution, the frequency of the ailment is at least as high as it is anywhere else.

(D) If high concentrations of many different pollutants in a city's air are correlated with a high frequency of the ailment among that city's population, then it is possible that two or more of those pollutants each causally contributes to the ailment.

(E) In cities in which there are high concentrations of many air pollutants, there are generally also high concentrations of other forms of pollution that are very likely to contribute causally to the ailment.

GO ON TO THE NEXT PAGE.

18. So far this summer there has been no rain in the valley. But usually a few inches of rain fall there each summer. Since only one week of summer is left, it will probably rain in the valley within the next week.

The flawed pattern of reasoning in the argument above is most similar to that in which one of the following arguments?

(A)   Aisha has finished proofreading all but the last two pages of an issue of the journal *Periodos* and has encountered no errors. However, there are sometimes a few errors in an issue of the journal *Periodos*. So there may be errors in the pages that Aisha has not yet checked.

(B)   There are generally few errors in an issue of the journal *Periodos*. Aisha has finished proofreading all but the last two pages of an issue of this journal but has encountered no errors. Hence, there are probably no errors in the pages that Aisha has not yet checked in this issue of the journal.

(C)   On average, there are a few errors in an issue of the journal *Periodos*. Aisha has finished proofreading all but the last two pages of an issue of this journal but has encountered no errors. So there are probably errors in the pages she has not yet checked in this issue of the journal.

(D)   Aisha has proofread several issues of the journal *Periodos* and has encountered no errors. But there are seldom any errors in an issue of this journal. So there will probably be no errors in the next issue of the journal *Periodos* that she proofreads.

(E)   There usually are errors in each issue of the journal *Periodos*. Since Aisha has finished proofreading the latest issue of this journal and has detected no errors, Aisha has probably made a mistake in her proofreading.

19. Young people believe efforts to reduce pollution, poverty, and war are doomed to failure. This pessimism is probably harmful to humanity's future, because people lose motivation to work for goals they think are unrealizable. We must do what we can to prevent this loss of motivation and therefore must enable our children to believe that better futures are possible.

Which one of the following is an assumption on which the argument depends?

(A)   Motivating people to work to solve humanity's problems will enable them to believe that the future can be better and will cause them to be less pessimistic.

(B)   Enabling people to believe that better futures are possible will help prevent the loss of motivation that results from pessimistic beliefs about the future.

(C)   Optimism about the future is better than pessimism, even if that optimism is based on an illusory vision of what is likely to occur.

(D)   If future generations believe that the future can be better, then pollution, poverty, and war will be eliminated.

(E)   The current prevalence of such problems as pollution and poverty stems from previous generations' inability to believe that futures can be better.

20. In a recent study of stroke patients, those who exhibited continuing deterioration of the nerve cells in the brain after the stroke also exhibited the highest levels of the protein glutamate in their blood. Glutamate, which functions within nerve cells as a neurotransmitter, can kill surrounding nerve cells if it leaks from damaged or oxygen-starved nerve cells. Thus glutamate leaking from damaged or oxygen-starved nerve cells is a cause of long-term brain damage resulting from strokes.

Which one of the following, if true, most strengthens the argument?

(A)   Any neurotransmitter that leaks from a damaged or oxygen-starved nerve cell will damage surrounding nerve cells.

(B)   Stroke patients exhibit a wide variety of abnormal chemical levels in their blood.

(C)   Glutamate is the only neurotransmitter that leaks from oxygen-starved or physically damaged nerve cells.

(D)   Leakage from damaged or oxygen-starved nerve cells is the only possible source of glutamate in the blood.

(E)   Nerve cells can suffer enough damage to leak glutamate without being destroyed themselves.

GO ON TO THE NEXT PAGE.

21. The only songs Amanda has ever written are blues songs and punk rock songs. Most punk rock songs involve no more than three chords. So if the next song Amanda writes is not a blues song, it probably will not involve more than three chords.

The reasoning in which one of the following arguments is most similar to that in the argument above?

(A)   The only pets the Gupta family has ever owned are fish and parrots. Most parrots are very noisy. So if the next pet the Gupta family owns is a parrot, it will probably be very noisy.

(B)   Most parrots are very noisy. The Gupta family has never owned any pets other than fish and parrots. So if the Gupta family has ever owned a noisy pet, it was probably a parrot.

(C)   All the pets the Gupta family has ever owned have been fish and parrots. Most parrots are very noisy. So any pet the Gupta family ever owns that is not a fish will probably be very noisy.

(D)   Every pet the Gupta family has ever owned has been a fish or a parrot. Most parrots are very noisy. So if the next pet the Gupta family owns is not a parrot, it will probably not be very noisy.

(E)   The Gupta family has never owned any pets other than fish and parrots. Most parrots are very noisy. So the next pet the Gupta family owns will probably be very noisy if it is not a fish.

22. Advertising tends to have a greater influence on consumer preferences regarding brands of yogurt than it does on consumer preferences regarding brands of milk. Yet, since the LargeCo supermarket chain began advertising its store-brand products, sales of its store-brand milk increased more than sales of its store-brand yogurt.

Which one of the following, if true, most helps to resolve the apparent discrepancy described above?

(A)   There has recently been increased demand at LargeCo stores for the chain's own brand of yogurt as well as for other brands of yogurt.

(B)   The typical shopper going to LargeCo for the purpose of buying milk does not go with the intention of also buying yogurt.

(C)   Shoppers at LargeCo tend to purchase the chain's own brand of dairy products more frequently than other brands of dairy products.

(D)   Supermarkets throughout the entire nation have experienced a sharp decrease in sales of yogurt recently.

(E)   Consumers tend to purchase store brands of yogurt, but purchase whichever brand of milk is least expensive.

23. Problem: If Shayna congratulates Daniel on his award, she will misrepresent her true feelings. However, if Shayna does not congratulate Daniel, she will hurt his feelings.

Principle: One should never be insincere about one's feelings, except possibly where one believes that the person with whom one is speaking would prefer kindness to honesty.

The principle, if valid, most helps to justify the reasoning in which one of the following arguments concerning the problem?

(A)   If Shayna congratulates Daniel, she will avoid hurting his feelings, so she should congratulate him.

(B)   Daniel might prefer for Shayna to congratulate him—even if insincerely—rather than for her to express her true feelings, and so Shayna would be doing nothing wrong in insincerely congratulating Daniel.

(C)   Shayna believes that kindness should be preferred to dishonesty when speaking to others, so she should not tell Daniel her true feelings.

(D)   Daniel's feelings would be hurt if he knew that congratulations from Shayna were insincere, so Shayna should not congratulate him.

(E)   Shayna has no opinion about whether Daniel would prefer kindness to honesty, so she should not congratulate him.

24. Clearly, a democracy cannot thrive without effective news media. After all, a democracy cannot thrive without an electorate that is knowledgeable about important political issues, and an electorate can be knowledgeable in this way only if it has access to unbiased information about the government.

The argument's conclusion is properly inferred if which one of the following is assumed?

(A)   All societies that have effective news media are thriving democracies.

(B)   If an electorate has access to unbiased information about the government, then that electorate will be knowledgeable about important political issues.

(C)   A democracy will thrive if its electorate is knowledgeable about important political issues.

(D)   A democracy cannot thrive if the electorate is exposed to biased information about the government.

(E)   Without effective news media, an electorate will not have access to unbiased information about the government.

GO ON TO THE NEXT PAGE.

25. Roberta is irritable only when she is tired, and loses things only when she is tired. Since she has been yawning all day, and has just lost her keys, she is almost certainly irritable.

The reasoning above is flawed in that it

(A) infers from a correlation between tiredness and yawning that tiredness causes yawning
(B) assumes the conclusion that it sets out to prove
(C) generalizes on the basis of a single instance
(D) takes a necessary condition for Roberta's losing things to be a sufficient condition
(E) takes a necessary condition for Roberta's being irritable to be a sufficient condition

26. Farmer: Crops genetically engineered to produce toxins that enable them to resist insect pests do not need to be sprayed with insecticides. Since excessive spraying of insecticides has harmed wildlife populations near croplands, using such genetically engineered crops more widely is likely to help wildlife populations to recover.

Which one of the following is an assumption the farmer's argument requires?

(A) Use of the crops that have been genetically engineered to resist insect pests in place of crops that have been sprayed with insecticides will cause less harm to wildlife populations.
(B) Wildlife populations that have been harmed by the excessive spraying of insecticides on croplands are likely to recover if the amount of insecticides sprayed on those croplands is reduced even slightly.
(C) Crops that have been genetically engineered to resist insect pests are never sprayed with insecticides that harm wildlife populations.
(D) Use of crops that have been genetically engineered to resist insect pests is no more costly to farmers than the use of insecticides on crops that are not genetically engineered.
(E) If a wider use of certain crops that have been genetically engineered to resist insect pests is likely to help at least some wildlife populations to recover, it is likely to have that effect only because its use will prevent excessive and ineffective spraying of insecticides on croplands.

S T O P

IF YOU FINISH BEFORE TIME IS CALLED, YOU MAY CHECK YOUR WORK ON THIS SECTION ONLY.
DO NOT WORK ON ANY OTHER SECTION IN THE TEST.

Wait for the supervisor's instructions before you open the page to the topic.
Please print and sign your name and write the date in the designated spaces below.

Time: 35 Minutes

General Directions

You will have 35 minutes in which to plan and write an essay on the topic inside. Read the topic and the accompanying directions carefully. You will probably find it best to spend a few minutes considering the topic and organizing your thoughts before you begin writing. In your essay, be sure to develop your ideas fully, leaving time, if possible, to review what you have written. **Do not write on a topic other than the one specified. Writing on a topic of your own choice is not acceptable.**

No special knowledge is required or expected for this writing exercise. Law schools are interested in the reasoning, clarity, organization, language usage, and writing mechanics displayed in your essay. How well you write is more important than how much you write.

Confine your essay to the blocked, lined area on the front and back of the separate Writing Sample Response Sheet. Only that area will be reproduced for law schools. Be sure that your writing is legible.

Both this topic sheet and your response sheet must be turned in to the testing staff before you leave the room.

Topic Code
127250

Date
/   /

Print Your Full Name Here		
Last	First	M.I.

Sign Your Name Here

Scratch Paper
Do not write your essay in this space.

LSAT® Writing Sample Topic

> Directions: The scenario presented below describes two choices, either one of which can be supported on the basis of the information given. Your essay should consider both choices and argue for one over the other, based on the two specified criteria and the facts provided. There is no "right" or "wrong" choice: a reasonable argument can be made for either.

A medium-sized company is located in a technology park in a sparsely populated area outside a major city. It has had difficulty retaining employees because of the long and expensive commute between the city and work that nearly all of its employees face. Consequently, the company will implement a commuting assistance plan. It must decide between operating a free bus for employees and subsidizing employees' costs of using public transportation. Using the facts below, write an essay in which you argue for one plan over the other based on the following two criteria:

- The company wants to minimize its employees' commuting expenses and frustrations.
- The company wants reliability and flexibility in its employees' work schedules.

Under the first plan, the company would lease a bus and hire a driver. The bus would make several daily circuits between the company's location and a single downtown stop, accessible by public transportation and close to a large, inexpensive parking garage. The only riders on the bus would be the company's employees. The bus has reclining seats and free Wi-Fi. The average total commute time for an employee would be 75 minutes each way. A breakdown of the bus would be disruptive to the company's operations.

Under the second plan, the company would partially reimburse employees' cost of using public transportation to commute to work. The average savings for an employee would be about 80 percent. Most of the employees live within walking distance to a bus stop. Most employees would have to make one or two transfers. Buses are scheduled to arrive every half hour at a bus shelter in the technology park. Buses are sometimes late. None of them have Wi-Fi. The average total commute time for an employee would be 60 minutes each way. WP-V127A

Scratch Paper
Do not write your essay in this space.

LAST
NAME
(Print)

L

LSAC ACCOUNT NO.

FIRST
NAME
(Print)

MI

TEST
CENTER NO.

SIGNATURE

LAST 4 DIGITS OF SOCIAL
SECURITY/SOCIAL
INSURANCE NO.

M M   D D   Y Y
TEST DATE

TOPIC CODE

Writing Sample Response Sheet

DO NOT WRITE
IN THIS SPACE

Begin your essay in the lined area below.
Continue on the back if you need more space.

COMPUTING YOUR SCORE

Directions:

1. Use the Answer Key on the next page to check your answers.

2. Use the Scoring Worksheet below to compute your raw score.

3. Use the Score Conversion Chart to convert your raw score into the 120–180 scale.

Scoring Worksheet

1. Enter the number of questions you answered correctly in each section.

	Number Correct
SECTION I	22 (-5)
SECTION II	21 (-4)
SECTION III	_____
SECTION IV	_____

2. Enter the sum here: _____
   This is your Raw Score.

Conversion Chart
For Converting Raw Score to the 120–180 LSAT Scaled Score
LSAT Form 4LSN110

Reported Score	Raw Score Lowest	Raw Score Highest
180	98	101
179	97	97
178	*	*
177	96	96
176	95	95
175	94	94
174	93	93
173	92	92
172	91	91
171	90	90
170	89	89
169	87	88
168	86	86
167	85	85
166	83	84
165	82	82
164	80	81
163	79	79
162	77	78
161	75	76
160	74	74
159	72	73
158	70	71
157	69	69
156	67	68
155	65	66
154	63	64
153	61	62
152	60	60
151	58	59
150	56	57
149	54	55
148	53	53
147	51	52
146	49	50
145	47	48
144	46	46
143	44	45
142	43	43
141	41	42
140	39	40
139	38	38
138	37	37
137	35	36
136	34	34
135	32	33
134	31	31
133	30	30
132	29	29
131	27	28
130	26	26
129	25	25
128	24	24
127	23	23
126	22	22
125	21	21
124	20	20
123	19	19
122	18	18
121	17	17
120	0	16

*There is no raw score that will produce this scaled score for this form.

ANSWER KEY

SECTION I

1.	A	8.	B	15.	B	22.	B
2.	B	9.	A	16.	C	23.	A
3.	D	10.	D	17.	B	24.	D
4.	B	11.	C	18.	E	25.	E
5.	A	12.	E	19.	A	26.	D
6.	E	13.	E	20.	E	27.	A
7.	C	14.	B	21.	A		

SECTION II

1.	C	8.	B	15.	B	22.	A
2.	E	9.	C	16.	A	23.	C
3.	A	10.	A	17.	B	24.	D
4.	D	11.	B	18.	E	25.	C
5.	D	12.	A	19.	B		
6.	D	13.	B	20.	E		
7.	C	14.	E	21.	E		

SECTION III

1.	B	8.	A	15.	D	22.	A
2.	C	9.	B	16.	D	23.	C
3.	B	10.	A	17.	B		
4.	E	11.	C	18.	E		
5.	E	12.	C	19.	A		
6.	D	13.	E	20.	B		
7.	A	14.	A	21.	E		

SECTION IV

1.	D	8.	D	15.	A	22.	D
2.	D	9.	D	16.	E	23.	E
3.	E	10.	E	17.	C	24.	E
4.	C	11.	B	18.	C	25.	E
5.	A	12.	A	19.	B	26.	A
6.	E	13.	B	20.	D		
7.	E	14.	C	21.	E		

LSAT® PREP TOOLS

NEW
10 Actual, Official LSAT PrepTests, Volume V™
(PrepTests 62–71)

It takes three years to produce enough PrepTests for a new 10 Actuals book! We are pleased to offer the latest in our 10 Actuals series: 10 Actual, Official LSAT PrepTests, Volume V. This new book is only the second in our 10 Actuals series to include previously administered Comparative Reading questions, which first appeared in the LSAT in 2007. This essential LSAT preparation tool encompasses PrepTest 62 (the December 2010 LSAT) through PrepTest 71 (the December 2013 LSAT).

For pure practice at an unbelievable price, you can't beat the 10 Actuals series. Each book includes:

• 10 previously administered LSATs
• an answer key for each test
• a writing sample for each test
• score-conversion tables

For the best value, purchase The Whole Test Prep Package V™, which includes the 10 Actual, Official LSAT PrepTests, Volume V, along with The Official LSAT SuperPrep® for only $38 (online only).

$24 Online

LSAC.org